"I Am the vine,
you are the branches."

John 15:5

JESUS THE WAYSHOWER

*Historical, Theological and Metaphysical Insights
into the Life and Teaching of the Master*

DAVID S. ALKINS

DIVIN BROOKS DIVINITY SCHOOL NTER
1819 East 14th Avenue
Denver, CO 80218-2603

Cover drawing: Judy Eyestone Daugherty, B.F.A.

Design: Bread & Butter Press, Denver.

The author especially wishes to thank:

Freda, his wife, without whom this book could not have been written;

Douglas Anderson, for his interest and expertise in editing;

Students and friends for their encouragement and support.

Library of Congress Catalog Card No. 83 - 090769

First Edition: 2000 Copies

Distributed by: DIVINE SCIENCE EDUCATIONAL CENTER
1819 East Fourteenth Avenue
Denver, Colorado 80218

BIBLE QUOTATIONS

Bible quotations are from the Authorized or King James Version. Other translations will be useful to the reader.

The Bible has been through many English translations. All are attempts to present the original text in language compatible with our Western culture. The ancient Hebrew mind used the oriental approach of expression. Sometimes this oriental approach resulted in vivid exaggerated word-pictures, both positive and negative, in order to make a lasting impression on the people of that time. Subsequent English translations serve to impart the kernel of truth that lies within the exaggerated form, thereby bringing forth the true significance of the teaching or event.

CORRESPONDENCE COURSE

This book comprises a home-study course (with written assignments for persons desiring to receive credit). It is available by correspondence through the Divine Science Educational Center. The Center also offers an advanced resident course—*The Life and Teaching of Jesus II*—taught by Dr. Alkins, with emphasis on Jesus' cosmic influence as The Christ. Persons wishing to enroll in either course are invited to contact the Registrar.

To

JESUS CHRIST

Who showed us

The Way

and to

MAURICE, MY FATHER

Who followed in

His Path

Preface

Divine Science, founded in 1898, is a Christian metaphysical teaching. It recognizes Jesus as the Christ. To have a true understanding of Divine Science one must have a knowledge of and an appreciation for the Christ Way of Life. The Christ Way of Life is exemplified in Jesus of Nazareth. To follow in his Way one must have a basic understanding of the principles that he taught and demonstrated.

This book is an *introduction* to Jesus' life and teaching. Historical, theological and metaphysical insights are presented in an attempt to give a *balanced* view of Jesus as Wayshower, for "as he is, so are we in this world." (I John 4:17)

Dr. Nona L. Brooks, co-founder of Divine Science, said that the primary blessings of life are to be realized by the practice of the spiritual principles that Jesus gave—"Seek ye first the Kingdom of God and His righteousness and all these things shall be added unto you." (Matthew 6:33)

"All these things," Jesus tells us, are the riches of the Kingdom of Heaven: the restoration of humanity's true dominion, the joy of direct communication with the Father through prayer and meditation resulting in peace of mind, supply, and all things needful to live a fruitful and fulfilled life on earth.

Jesus became the enabler of his own teaching through his spiritual work in union with the Father. Through his activation of the Holy Spirit into the race consciousness he blazed a trail for us to follow that will set us free from all forms of limitation.

The culmination of Christian living is victory and overcoming, accompanied by the willingness to give oneself to the Sovereign Will of God in all things. Using the Bible as the basic text, Divine Science focuses on the teaching of Jesus as it shows forth the principles of our own unfoldment of the Indwelling Christ. "But we all, with open face beholding as in a glass the glory of the Lord, are changed into the same image from glory to glory, even as by the Spirit of the Lord." (II Corinthians 3:18)

That Grand Design of the Universe was individualized to the fullest in Jesus the Wayshower. It is that jewel of Truth that lies at the heart of life, and it is individualized in each of us—but it remains to be discovered and applied.

Through study, prayer and meditation, this book may serve to open up your spirit, "For it is God which worketh in you both to will and to do of His good pleasure." (Philippians 2:13)

David S. Alkins

Contents

JESUS' PRAYER FOR US

*I pray for them . . . for they are thine, I have
given them thy word. They are not of the world
even as I am not of the world. Sanctify (perfect)
them through thy truth: thy word is truth. And for
their sakes I sanctify myself, that they also might
be sanctified (perfected) through the truth. That
they all may be one; as thou, Father, art in me,
and I in thee, that they also may be one in us . . .*

John 17:9, 14, 16, 17, 19, 21

CHAPTER I

In the Fullness of the Times

Jesus appeared on the human scene in what the Apostle Paul called "the fullness of the times." While Eternity is not confined to time and space, the work of earth moves within Divine timeframes. "The fullness of the times" does not mean that the consciousness of mankind was in a state of readiness to receive the Christ, for history shows that it rejected him. Because of humanity's great need, because it had lost its awareness of union with God, it became immobilized—what the Bible calls "gross darkness, with ears waxed shut and eyes that could not see." God in His great love for us sent One who was to become fully aware of His Divine Indwelling. Thus Jesus of Nazareth, in union with the Father, became "the Word made flesh" (John 1:14), the Light, the Wayshower, the Christ. To understand the impact of Jesus' work on the consciousness of that time, we need to acquire insights into the significance of this immobolized state.

HISTORICAL AND POLITICAL INSIGHTS

The small country that we know as Palestine today had known the oppression of many foreign aggressors. Centuries before the birth of Christ, a large segment of the Jewish population had been carried off to captivity in Babylon, leaving a small remnant behind to live amongst the ruins and the result of war. Of this remnant many intermarried with other cultures and eventually lost their national and religious identity. The Babylonian captives eventually became captives of Persia when Babylon was defeated by Cyrus of Persia in 539 B.C. These new captors, in fulfillment of Bible prophecy (Isaiah 45), were actually to become benefactors. Eventually they provided the way for the Jews to return to their homeland, rebuild their temple in Jerusalem, and continue their way of life in Palestine.

There came a day, however, when the beneficent rulers were gone and, with the ascendance of Artaxerxes III to the Persian throne, a new oppression began for the Jewish people.

Hungry for power, Artaxerxes (also known as Xerxes) covetously sought control over Europe. In the world of duality, where power is pitted against power, new aggressors always appear on the scene. Xerxes was defeated by the Athenians (Greeks) and driven back to Asia. Philip, a brilliant military leader who had seized the throne of Macedon in Greece (359 B.C.), had planned a massive attack on Xerxes in Asia Minor but was assassinated before he could undertake his mission. The cause was successfully undertaken by his son, Alexander the Great, who went on to conquer Egypt, the eastern Mediterranean world, Persia, and, with it, Palestine. Alexander, a student of Aristotle, had a great longing to extend the Greek culture throughout his empire.

Alexander the Great did not live to see his dream fulfilled. He died at age 32. Some of his army commanders partitioned his empire, each ruling a portion of it. One of them was Seleucus Nicator, who became the ruler of Babylonia in 312 B.C. His empire became known as Syria. Another segment of Alexander's conquests was taken by Ptolemy I, who ruled Egypt and Palestine. With a continual struggle for power going on between the Seleucid and Ptolemy dynasties, the Jews were subjected to one group and then another.

Years later, the Seleucid ruler Antiochus III came to power; he sought to impose the total Greek culture upon the Jews. In addition he levied higher taxes and deposed the rightful (Jewish) high priest, replacing him with a Jewish traitor who in effect "bought" the ecclesiastical office in exchange for supporting Antiochus' demands. When the Jews resisted, a great wave of persecution broke out. Under penalty of death, Jews were forbidden to engage in their religious practices, copies of the Mosaic Law were destroyed, and an altar to the Greek god Zeus was erected in the Jews' beloved temple in Jerusalem. The face of Zeus was actually the face of Antiochus himself. Pigs were offered on the altar; and elsewhere throughout the country, pagan altars were erected and the Jews were forced to pay homage to the Greek gods.

A revolt began as a few of the stronger-willed Jews were determined to remain faithful to the One True God—the God who had been proclaimed through their ancestors, Abraham, Moses and the prophets. An aged Jewish priest named Mattathias and his five sons became leaders of what came to be known as the Maccabean Revolt. The religious freedom and peace following the success of the Maccabean Revolt was to be short-lived and Palestine was to know new aggressors.

The Syrian armies marched on the land and brought it under control of Syria. Again the Jews were forced to pay high tribute money to their conquerors. At the same time, ecclesiastical and political struggles were going on within the ranks of the religious authorities of Judaism, to the extent that bloodshed and murder occurred within families of priestly authority in their quest for power.

While these power struggles were going on within Judaism, Rome was steadily on the march. The great Roman general Pompey eventually conquered Syria and, with that, Palestine came under the dominion of Rome. In 63 B.C., Jerusalem, which resisted the Roman occupation, was defeated but not without merciless bloodshed. Thousands of Jews were killed by Pompey; then, out of sheer curiosity, he entered the holy of holies of their temple. This was an outrage to the Jews but they were helpless to throw off the shackles of Roman power.

In the years that followed, an Idumaean named Antipater possibly saved Julius Caesar's life while effectively fighting against a large Egyptian army. Caesar repaid Antipater by granting him many requests. Antipater continued to gain favor from Rome even after Caesar's death.

Antipater's son, Herod, was eventually to remind the Roman Senate of his father's friendship with Caesar and persuade them to name him king of Judea. Herod was completely egocentric, stopping at nothing to gain power. He even killed his own sons when he felt they were in his way. The Bible tells us that Herod ordered the slaughter of innocent babies when he learned of the birth of Christ and feared that another earthly ruler had come upon the scene. This merciless

killing was done out of a crazed fear that the prophesied King
of the Jews (the Messiah) would take away his throne.

RELIGIOUS AND PHILOSOPHICAL INSIGHTS

From Abraham and his descendents, the Jews, came forth a
great statement of Truth: "The Lord our God is ONE"—
monotheism. Throughout their history the Jews preserved the
awareness of this universal truth. The central core of Judaism
remained faithful to this revelation and had nothing to do with
the pagan religious practices, which were cruel and sadistic rites
to a plurality of cruel and sadistic gods.

When the Greek culture was imposed upon them by
Alexander's successors, they resisted this Hellenization process
insofar as it contradicted the religious truths they had
maintained throughout their history. The Hellenistic Age
brought Greek art, athletics, science and religious practices to
the countries conquered by Greece. There was much beauty
and enlightenment in all of this, but also many deterrents to
spiritual growth. Beautiful expressions through art forms are
worthy of admiration and attention, but when they become
ends in themselves they impede the soul journey.

The philosophical approach, where the human reasoning
faculty had dominance, was at the root of Greek thought. The
problems and issues of life were dealt with on the basis of
deduction and logic, the faculties of the conscious mind. With
philosophy separated from religious life, rational thinking
maintained the primacy of activity. The religious mind, on the
other hand, would have the rational and deductive reasoning
mind become more passive, while awaiting the inner revelation
of Truth from the voice of God within the soul. All the good in
Greek philosophy pointed to a Primal Cause behind the
universe. Logic and reasoning told them that motion must be
controlled by a "Prime Mover," but the intellect of the Greeks
could not bring them into an EXPERIENCE of the Living God,
nor could they begin to describe God's nature as Love. Carried
to an extreme, the intellect can actually rationalize God away
completely.

With their many anthropomorphic deities, the Greeks attributed lesser human qualities to their gods. They became angry or jealous and they warred with one another. In short, they were filled with human egocentric emotions. Paul was to note in Athens an altar to what the Greeks called "an unknown god." He noted superstition (a degenerative power of mind) in their understanding and he revealed the great truth to the "Men of Athens" that in God "we live and move and have our being." God was not separate and apart from His creation but one with it.

Fear of death was prevalent during Jesus' time. For the Greeks there was Hades, the fearful god of the underworld, and the dog-headed monster that prevented the soul from ever leaving Hades' domain. The Jews, despite the fact that they had attained to the highest degree of Truth at that time, also had a fear of the dreaded Sheol, an abode of the dead. Job described it as "the land of darkness and the shadow of death. A land of darkness, as darkness itself; and of the shadow of death, without any order, and where the light is as darkness." (Job 10:21,22) Job said that from that abode he would not return.

The Jewish religious concepts had degenerated into bondage through extreme legalism by the time Jesus was born. The emphasis was on fear of God rather than love for God. There was forced obedience to the Law, and adherence to the Law had become cause-centered rather than person-centered. With their attention fixed on the Cause of the Law, there was much dissecting and analyzing over the "letter of the law." The intent of the Law was buried under the debris of legalism.

The Pentateuch (the first five books of the Old Testament) was the Law of Moses for the Jewish people. The Pentateuch contained 614 rules that had to do with right conduct in daily living. In order to secure God's blessing, Jesus found the Pharisees going through all sorts of complicated rites and rituals. This great emphasis on the externals of religion caused the truth of the activity of God within to become hidden and dormant. Thus the center of contact—the means of EXPERIENCING the Presence of God—was cut off. The inherent function of the Law of Moses had been broken apart and dissected. Attainment was through striving and straining to keep the Law by way of willpower alone, rather than by allowing God to express through the individual. With such a severe analysis there were many detours in the Jewish religious life that led to dead ends. They were not only under the bondage of Rome without, but even worse, they were captive to the bondage of legalism within.

THE IMMOBILIZED CONSCIOUSNESS

This was the period of the immobilized consciousness. Aggressors seeking worldly power were on the move, diverting creative energies into a driving, consuming desire for outer gain. Human life and welfare was of little concern to this lust for power. The dominated ones, on the other hand, felt a complete sense of hopelessness to combat this aggression. Continual demands of taxation were made upon the Jews by their conquerors. They were denied their God-given right of freedom. They could not even look to their religious leaders for comfort and strength, except in rare instances, for the priesthood had been desecrated. Religious authorities used their offices for their own selfish purposes and held the common people in spiritual bondage. The product of Hebrew worship was a vindictive God of judgment, a God afar off, not near at hand. The truth that mankind was created in the "image and after the likeness" of God was becoming lost. God was sought through the avenue of willpower, of obedience to the external aspects of the Law, rather than through inner knowledge and awareness. Soul growth had come to a halt because of the striving to attain.

In working with the will alone, the latent soul faculties were becoming dormant through lack of stimulation and use. The underlying error was that the personality, through sheer work and willpower, must overcome, rather than realize that it is only through God within (the awareness of His Divine Indwelling) that attainments can be made. Spiritual vision was so distorted that it prevented the rising consciousness from beholding the Living God.

On the whole, mankind had turned away from God. As was voiced by the Prophet Jeremiah hundreds of years before, "my people have . . . forsaken me, the fountain of living waters, and hewed them out cisterns, broken cisterns, that can hold no water." (Jer. 2:13)

Even the thought of death proved to be no escape from the dread of living, for as Job in his unillumined state voices, "There is hope of a tree if it be cut down that it will sprout again . . . but when man dieth and wasteth away, yea when man giveth up the ghost where is he? As the waters fail from the sea, and the flood decayeth and drieth up: so man lieth down and riseth not: till the heavens be no more, they shall not awake, nor be raised out of their sleep." (Job 14: 7, 10-12)

In this deluge of hopelessness, one hope did prevail—the fulfillment of the prophecies which promised the coming of a Deliverer, the Messiah, who would break this pattern of bondage. The Prophet Isaiah had proclaimed the office and mission of the Messiah: "The Spirit of the Lord God is upon me; because the Lord hath anointed me to preach good tidings unto the meek; he hath sent me to bind up the brokenhearted, to proclaim liberty to the captives, and the opening of the prison to them that are bound; to proclaim the acceptable year of the Lord, and the day of vengeance of our God; to comfort all that mourn; to appoint unto them that mourn in Zion, to give unto them beauty for ashes, the oil of joy for mourning, the garment of praise for the spirit of heaviness; that they might be called trees of righteousness, the planting of the Lord, that he might be glorified." (Is. 61:1-3)

In this setting of the immobilized consciousness—one of covetous, greedy aggressors seeking a worldly kingdom, of religious leaders who sought only self-aggrandizement, of hopelessness for the common people—the Prince of Peace was born—the One who would deny himself all worldly power and give his life to bring the Kingdom of God into visible manifestation on earth.

In humble birth, in simple surroundings, Jesus arrived and demonstrated the spiritual power of humility. He laid down his life for the world, in order that humankind might know the Truth that sets us free, and see the manifest power of God.

17

CHAPTER II

Prophecy Relating to Jesus

Before the advent of Jesus Christ the consciousness was at a very low ebb. There were power struggles within the secular world as one aggressor overcame another, only to open the way for other aggressors to follow. There were also power struggles within the Judaic religious framework as egocentric leaders vied for positions of high authority. Emphasis was on attainment through willpower in adhering to the letter of the Mosaic Law; and worship had been reduced to intricate exercises of ritual and ceremony. The oppressed felt a sense of hopelessness, with no way to secure freedom from their oppressors. They had not been taught and trained in the atmosphere of a God of Love who is always and everywhere available. They understood, when at their best, that God was "a very present help in trouble" (Ps. 46), but they did not have the full realization of Omnipresence and the power of His Divine Indwelling.

Only one hope prevailed to those who looked to God for deliverance in those days. This was the hope of the coming Messiah who had been prophesied throughout the Old Testament. Beginning with Genesis, a generalized prophetic promise was made to Abraham that from his seed should all the families of the world be blessed. (Gen. 12:3; 26:4, et al) This covenant with Abraham was said to be an Everlasting one, indicating the ongoing spiritual blessings to come from it. These promises became more specific as the tribe of Judah was named as the one out of which the Messiah would come. Moses was also to speak of this coming Prophet, and years later Samuel would also refer to the "faithful priest."

With the ongoing prophecy there was continued specificity— the Deliverer would come from the house of David of the tribe of Judah. The author of the 22nd Psalm became so at one with the prophecy that he actually prophesied the rejection of the Messiah, as well as his death. Psalm 22 opens with "My God, my God, why hast thou forsaken me?," which were Jesus' dying words on the Cross. It continues with "they pierced my hands and my feet and cast lots upon my vesture."

As time went on, Isaiah prophesied, "Therefore the Lord himself shall give you a SIGN: Behold, a virgin shall conceive and bear a son, and shall call his name Emmanuel (God with us) . . . . " (Isa. 7:14) "And he shall be for a sanctuary, but for a stone of stumbling and for a rock of offence to both the houses of Israel" (Judah and Benjamin). (Isa. 8:14) "For unto us a child is born, unto us a son is given: and the government shall be upon his shoulder and his name shall be called Wonderful Counsellor, The Mighty God, The Everlasting Father, the Prince of Peace. Of the increase of his government and peace there shall be no end, upon the throne of David and upon his kingdom, to order it, and to establish it with judgment and with justice from henceforth even forever. The zeal of the Lord of hosts will perform this." (Isa. 9:6,7) "And there shall come forth a rod out of the stem of Jesse (David's father) and a Branch shall grow out of his roots and the spirit of the Lord shall rest upon him, the spirit of wisdom and understanding, the spirit of counsel and might (spiritual strength), the spirit of knowledge and of the fear (respect) of the Lord. And I shall make him of quick understanding in the fear of the Lord; and he shall not judge after the sight of his eyes, neither reprove after the hearing of his ears; but with righteousness shall he judge the poor and reprove with equity for the meek of the earth . . . ." (Isa. 11:1-4) "And in that day there shall be a root of Jesse, which shall stand for an ensign of the people; to it shall the Gentiles seek and his Rest shall be glorious." (Isa. 11:10)

Isaiah specifically prophesies the work of John the Baptist as the forerunner of Christ: "The voice of him that crieth in the wilderness, Prepare ye the way of the Lord, make straight in the desert a highway for our God. Every valley shall be exalted, and every mountain and hill shall be made low: and the crooked shall be made straight, and the rough places plain: and the glory of the Lord shall be revealed, and all flesh shall see it together: for the mouth of the Lord hath spoken it." (Isa. 40:3-5) And of the Messiah he said, "He shall feed his flock like a shepherd: he shall gather the lambs with his arm, and carry them in his bosom, and shall gently lead those that are with young." (Isa. 40:11)

Jesus himself quoted a passage from the Book of Isaiah (Luke 4:16-21) which described the office of the Christ and he said that he himself was the fulfillment of that prophecy. The Prophets Jeremiah and Daniel also picked up the theme of the coming of the Messiah. The Prophet Micah pinpoints the birthplace of the Christ in these words: "But thou Bethlehem Ephratah, though thou be little among the thousands of Judah, yet out of thee shall come forth unto me that is to be ruler in Israel: whose goings forth have been from of old, from everlasting." (Micah 5:2)

The Prophet Zechariah foretells the betrayal of Christ by Judas Iscariot. "And I said unto them, If ye think good, give me my price; and if not, forbear. So they weighed for my price thirty pieces of silver. And the Lord said unto me, Cast it unto the potter; a goodly price that I was prised at of them. And I took the thirty pieces of silver, and cast them to the potter in the house of the Lord." (Zech. 11:12,13)

The last of the Old Testament writings is that of the Prophet Malachi. He describes the forerunner of the Christ, John the Baptist (or Baptizer), as well as the Christ suddenly appearing. "Behold, I will send my messenger, and he shall prepare the way before me: and the Lord, whom ye seek, shall suddenly come to his temple, even the messenger of the covenant, whom ye delight in: behold, he shall come, saith the Lord of hosts . . . he is like a refiner's fire and like fullers' sope." (Mal. 3:1-3) The Old Testament closes with Malachi's words, "Behold, I will send you Elijah the prophet before the coming . . . of the day of the Lord, and he shall turn the heart of the fathers to the children, and the heart of the children to their fathers." (Mal. 4:5,6) John the Baptist was described by these words in the Gospels as the one to fulfill that prophecy, who came in the spirit of Elijah. (Luke 1:17; Matt. 11:10-15, et al)

Not only did the Jewish religious literature carry prophecies and information concerning the Messiah, but the Gentile literature, hundreds of years before the birth of Christ, announced his coming. Emma Curtis Hopkins, the great "teacher of the teachers" in New Thought, reports in her book *High Mysticism* that 1800 years before the birth of the Christ, Zoroaster in Persia wrote about a star that would appear at midday to announce that a virgin had conceived and born a son. Zoroaster advised his readers to follow that star wherever it would lead them, for through it they would be led to this "mysterious Child." In humility they should offer him gifts— for their homage would be paid to one whom Zoroaster described as "the Almighty Word . . . your Lord and Everlasting King." (*High Mysticism*, page 99)

Thus we have some interesting insights into the coming of the Wise Men or Magi from the East. The Magi believed that a star had the qualities of being a "fravashi"—the angel or the counterpart of great personages. The Book of Numbers records such an understanding of the Messiah. "There shall come a Star out of Jacob (Israel) and a sceptre (King) shall rise out of Israel." (Num. 24:17-19)

Emma Curtis Hopkins goes on to record the writings of others, recorded hundreds of years before Jesus' birth. The prophecy of the Chaldeans described him as "the Lofty One to arrive among men." To those seers of the Egyptians he was described as "the Lord of the whole world." The Chinese foresaw his mission as "the Saving One" who would be born and then who would "die for the race." The Sibyls considered him to be a "Saviour" coming to reveal the Truth to mankind of its own "God Nature," thereby redeeming it. Writing 750 years before Christ, the Erythrean Sibyl foresaw the details of his rejection by man, relating that he would be killed by being hanged on a tree, he would be given gall and vinegar to drink. At the time of his dying there would be three hours darkness lasting from midday; but that he would rise on the third day, and, "all who acknowledge Him king shall be happy in His kingdom." (*High Mysticism*, page 124) These ancient prophetic events were fulfilled as Jesus died on the Cross and demonstrated the Resurrection on the third day after his death.

In pre-announcing this important birth, the secular, the scientific (Magi) and the religious world had all been told of the Messiah's coming. Because all the literature indicated that he would possess God-Power, those in positions of temporal power (such as King Herod), as well as those in positions of ecclesiastical power (the high priests, the scribes and Pharisees), were to see this special Birth as a real threat to their vested interests. And so the Apostle John says that "he came unto his own and his own received him not." (John 1:11) *"But as many as received him, to them gave he power to become the sons of God*, even to them that believe on his name: which were born, not of blood, nor of the will of the flesh, nor of the will of man, but of God. And the Word was made flesh, and dwelt among us . . . ." (John 1:12-14) Jesus as the Word (God) in physical manifestation shows forth the inherent divinity of all mankind. As the Christ of God he became the Wayshower to bring everyone into the awareness of their Divine heritage.

READ: Isaiah 9:2-7; 42:1-10; 52:13-15; all of Chapter 53; 61:1-3. Jeremiah 23:5,6. Daniel 7:13,14; 9:24-26. Micah 5:2-4; Zechariah 3:8; 9:9; 12:10.
These are but a few of the Old Testament prophecies concerning the Christ.

Optional reading: Emma Curtis Hopkins, *High Mysticism*, p. 99 and p. 124. Pub.: DeVorss & Co., P.O. Box 550, Marina del Rey, CA 90291

CHAPTER III

Ramifications of His Birth

The four Gospels of the New Testament—Matthew, Mark, Luke and John—give us the most complete source of information on the life and teaching of Jesus. The Book of the Acts of the Apostles (written by Luke) is also a rich embellishment of the manifested demonstrations coming forth from Jesus' teaching through Spirit-enablement. Aside from these sacred writings there were also secular writers who related some valuable insights into Jesus' life. Among these are the writings of Josephus, a Jewish officer in the war with the Romans (A.D. 66–70); and the Roman historian, Tacitus.

A careful reading of the Gospels indicates that these writers were eyewitnesses of his work and teaching. Matthew and John were of the original twelve disciples. Mark was a young boy whose parents received Jesus and his disciples into their home. Mark has been known as Peter's recorder. It is believed that Peter dictated the Gospel of Mark to young Mark. Luke was a Gentile physician who undoubtedly was very close to Jesus' mother, Mary, receiving much vital information from her. He writes that Mary pondered all these things and kept them in her heart, (Luke 2:19, 51) inferring that these ponderings were revealed to Luke for written transmission in Divine timing. Luke is the only Gospel writer who gives any insights into Jesus' youth. This information must have been given to him by Mary. Although Luke was not one of the original twelve disciples, he indicates that he was an eyewitness of many of the events and received all his information from valid sources. The opening of his Gospel states: "Forasmuch as many have taken in hand to set forth in order a declaration of those things which are most surely believed among us, even as they delivered them unto us, *which from the beginning were eyewitnesses, and ministers of the word;* it seemed good *to me also, having had perfect understanding of all things from the very first,* to write unto thee in order, most excellent Theophilus, that thou mightest know *the certainty of those things*, wherein thou has been instructed." (Luke 1:1-4)

THE BIRTH

At the time of the birth of Christ, we have noted that Palestine was under the domination of Rome. Because the tyranny of bondage and taxation was so great, there were varying ideas as to how to throw off the shackles of the oppressor; but for many, a sense of despair and hopelessness prevailed until the Deliverer should be born.

Generally speaking, there was a lack of agreement among the Jews as to how they should resist and overcome. The Essenes, a religious sect, felt that it was best to withdraw from the world and give themselves over to prayer and contemplation, and thus spiritually prepare for the coming of the Messiah. The Dead Sea Scrolls reveal much of their spiritual work.

Working from the other extreme, a group of Jewish patriots called the Zealots felt that they should resort to violence in order to relieve their people from bondage. While they were also Messiah-oriented, it was their intent to cooperate with their image of the Messiah (a nationalistic, military leader) in an armed rebellion against Rome.

Between these two extremes—the Essenes and the Zealots—were the Sadducees, Pharisees and scribes. The Sadducees represented the Jewish aristocracy, very worldly and politically oriented. The scribes were a group of Jewish scholars who had so analyzed and dissected the Mosaic Law that they actually had taken away the key to spiritual understanding and knowledge. The Pharisees, with their emphasis on numerous outer observances and insistence on living the "letter of the Law," could offer no spiritual aid in coping with living experiences.

"In the fullness of the times"—in Divine timing when God saw mankind's dilemma and helplessness—the Deliverer, the Messiah—Christ was born. According to our calendar Jesus was probably born in the Roman year 747 or 6 B.C. Every Christmas we hear the well-known events—the announcement of his birth to a Hebrew maiden named Mary, and her question, "How shall this thing be, seeing that I know no man?," pointing to a work of a greater dimension of Spirit than had been demonstrated to that point in time or since. She was told that her conception would be in this fashion: "The Holy Ghost shall come upon thee, and the power of the Highest shall overshadow thee: therefore also that holy thing which shall be born of thee shall be called the Son of God." (Luke 1:26-35) Mary realized a great expansion in consciousness—the limitless activity of God which is not bound to matter, nor to human means of reproduction. The Bible treats the Birth in this manner.

While Mary could accept that "with God nothing shall be impossible" in this matter (Luke 1:37), Joseph had some real struggle with it. Matthew records Joseph's dilemma: "Now the birth of Jesus Christ was on this wise: When as his mother Mary was espoused (engaged) to Joseph, before they came together, she was found with child of the Holy Ghost. Then Joseph her (espoused) husband, being a just man, and not willing to make her a publick example, was minded to put her away privily." Engagement was as binding as a marriage vow in that culture. To break an engagement had the same impact as going through a divorce. The fact that Mary was pregnant prior to the physical consummation of their marriage was a great social disgrace. An unjust man would have publicly proclaimed his innocence in the matter and left the woman to suffer the consequences. However, Joseph had compassion on her and wanted to secretly send her away to have the baby, breaking the engagement. "While he thought on these things, behold, the angel of the Lord appeared unto him in a dream, saying, Joseph, thou son of David, fear not to take unto thee Mary thy wife: for that which is conceived in her is of the Holy Ghost. And she shall bring forth a son, and thou shalt call his name JESUS: for he shall save his people from their sins. Now all this was done, that it might be fulfilled which was spoken of the Lord by the prophet (Isaiah), saying, Behold, a virgin shall be with child, and shall bring forth a son, and they shall call his name Emmanuel, which being interpreted is, God with us. Then Joseph being raised from sleep did as the angel of the Lord had bidden him, and took unto him his wife: and knew her not till she had brought forth her firstborn son: and he called his name JESUS." (Matt. 1:18-25)

The Bible records the physical aspects of Jesus' birth as unique. The birth was heralded by a mysterious conjunction of the cosmic world—a tremendous star which moved through the heavens leading scientific investigators to the child. Humble shepherds on the outskirts of Bethlehem experienced a clairaudient experience from celestial beings who made the announcement of the great event. This was accompanied by the music of the spheres (angels) giving glory to God and pronouncing peace on earth to men of good will. This is a tremendous occurrence, but its telling from year to year has become so commonplace that for many it has lost its significance.

The impact of this particular birth divided history into B.C. and A.D., and changed the course of human events. Mankind's awareness was lifted beyond the confines of the three-dimensional world into the world of Spirit. The Holy Spirit (the grace of God in activity) was quickened and released into the world consciousness. Our true nature and our relationship with God was proclaimed. That we were meant to have dominion, even over death itself, was mediated through the Master. He brought liberation to mankind by making that liberation from *within* rather than through human struggle from without. He pointed to the Eternal source of supply, gave us the key to release from earth bondage, declared Divine protection, and showed the way to the abiding and established consciousness of the Kingdom of Heaven on earth, where "all these things shall be added unto you."

After the birth of her baby, Mary followed the customs of that culture in wrapping the child in swaddling clothes. These were long strips of linen which bound the infant's arms and legs tightly. If babies were bound in this fashion for at least six months it was believed that their limbs would grow straight.

Another custom of those times was that a mother was considered "unclean" for 40 days after the birth of a son and even longer after the birth of a daughter. She was confined either to her home or to places where she would not be around other people. After her period of confinement, Mary, Joseph and Jesus made a visit to the Temple and made a sacrificial offering of two turtle doves, the least expensive of the required offerings. This is an indication that they were not wealthy people. These offerings were purchased outside the Temple from merchants who had profiteered and built up a rich business enterprise, taking advantage of those who had a desire to know the favor of God by way of sacrificial offerings. Jesus was later to show that they who worship God need not promote the vested interests of these merchants, but that the true worshipper would know God in Spirit and in Truth.

While Mary, Joseph and the infant Jesus were in the Temple for the ceremony of the Purification of Women after childbirth, they encountered a very devout and illumined man named Simeon. He took Jesus in his arms and voiced his illumination concerning the baby as he blessed God: "Lord, now lettest thou thy servant depart in peace, according to thy word: For mine eyes have seen thy salvation. Which thou hast prepared before the face of all people; a light to lighten the Gentiles, and the glory of thy people Israel." (Luke 2:25-32) He then prophesied to Mary, "Behold this child is set for the fall and rising again of many in Israel; and for a sign which shall be spoken against; (Yea, a sword shall pierce through thy own soul also,) that the thoughts of many hearts may be revealed." (Luke 2:34,35)

Simeon was not the only devotee of God who was to recognize Jesus' mission. There was a very aged woman named Anna who never left the Temple, but stayed there constantly fasting and praying. When she saw Jesus she gave thanks and spoke "of him to all them that looked for redemption in Jerusalem." (Luke 2:36-38)

King Herod, appointed by the Romans to rule over the Jews, received the news of this birth in a very different manner than did Simeon and Anna. When the king learned through the Wise Men (Magi) that they were seeking the "one that is born King of the Jews," Herod became insane with fear and greed, and sought to prevent anyone from taking his throne. He issued a decree that every male child two years of age and under should be destroyed. This merciless slaughter of innocent children was recorded by the Prophet Jeremiah hundreds of years before: "In Rama was there a voice heard, lamentation, and weeping, and great mourning, Rachel weeping for her children, and would not be comforted, because they are not." (Matt. 2:16-18) Rachel, the favorite wife of the Patriarch Jacob (who was renamed Israel) is symbolized in this writing of Jeremiah as the mother of the nation of Israel.

Joseph received a dream from God warning him of Herod's plans. Divine instructions were given to take the child and his mother and go into Egypt so that Jesus would be spared from this massacre. The angel who spoke to Joseph in that dream told him that they would receive further guidance as to when it was safe to return to their homeland. Again another prophecy was fulfilled, which said "Out of Egypt have I called my son." (Matt 2:12-15)

The promised guidance came after the death of King Herod. Herod's son, Archelaus, had become king of Judea, and Joseph realized that Judea would not be a safe place to live. The family received guidance directing them to the land of Galilee to make their home. Nazareth in Galilee had been their original home and so they returned to that town, which fulfilled the prophecy, "He shall be called a Nazarene." (Matt. 2:19-23)

By that time the Romans had divided Palestine into five provinces: Galilee, Samaria, Judea, Idumea and Perea. Herod, their puppet-king, had not been a true Jew, but an Idumean. A century before Herod's birth his ancestors had been part of a forced conversion to Judaism. After Herod's death his kingdom was divided amongst his three living sons, Herod Antipas, Philip and Archelaus. While they were not as cruel as their father, they nevertheless followed many of his policies.

Galilee and Perea were ruled by Herod Antipas. Since Joseph and Mary were directed to make their home in this province, it can be inferred that he was a milder ruler than his brother Archelaus, who ruled Judea, Samaria and Idumea. Rome eventually removed Archelaus from office and sent a military governor to rule in his place. The third brother, Philip, ruled the lands north and east of the Sea of Galilee and eventually built the beautiful, Greek-styled city of Caesarea Philippi.

HISTORICAL AND METAPHYSICAL INSIGHTS

We must never lose sight of the fact that the birth of Jesus was an actual, historical happening, fulfilling God's plans for earth, manifesting in Divine time-lines, through the agency of human flesh. Nevertheless, until he (the Christ) is born afresh in us, until the Holy Birth takes place in our awareness, we cannot benefit personally.

The birth of the Christ within us through the unfoldment of our divine natures (II Peter 1:1-8) causes the Divine Idea to emerge within our consciousness. Since unillumined man cannot understand the things of the Spirit, we must guard these sacred, inner illuminations from the "Herods" of this world. Sharing of spiritual experiences with those not yet ready in consciousness to understand them results in rejection, even condemnation. At this point dualism enters: often human reasoning, deduction and logic (tools of the three dimensional world) wash away spiritual experiences. It is better to take these insights down into "Egypt" where they may be protected. One of the metaphysical meanings of Egypt is "shut in," signifying the darkness of obscurity. When the time is right—when we receive that inner guidance from the Father—we may manifest these ideas. Until we receive the guidance, it is better that such ideas be nurtured through prayer, meditation and contemplation in the silence of the soul, so that they may become fixed, settled and established in consciousness.

A study of the Bible shows that Jesus' life paralleled the history of the Israelites in many instances. Hundreds of years before, during a great famine in Canaan, the Patriarch Jacob, who became Israel, went into Egypt with his large family in order to survive. The Israelites stayed there for many generations, eventually coming under the bondage of the Egyptian pharoahs. However, when the time was right the Exile occurred. Moses brought the children of Israel "out of the house of bondage" and into the Land of Canaan. In his infancy Jesus was hidden and protected in Egypt, paralleling that same protection that was given Jacob during the famine.

Jesus' mastery of life experiences was always of short duration compared with that of the Israelites. For example, his wilderness experience in his early manhood was mastered in 40 days, whereas the Israelites were 40 years in the wilderness, and only some of them overcame their circumstances.

We watch the Law of Expression in action as manifested positively in Jesus. Conversely, it manifested negatively in the aged tyrant, Herod. His final years were spent in agony, his mind tortured by insanity and his body wracked with disease. Paul relates the positive and negative aspects of the Law of Expression as he contrasts the Mosaic Law (the working at soul mastery through willpower alone), with the Christ Way of Life. The culminating process is "the mystery which hath been hid from ages and from generations, but now is made manifest . . . CHRIST IN YOU, the hope of glory." (Col. 1:26,27)

Paul made a contrast in the Law and the work of the unfolding Holy Spirit: "If the ministration of death, written and engraven in stones, was glorious, so that the children of Israel could not steadfastly behold the face of Moses for the glory of his countenance; which glory was to be done away: How shall not the ministration of the spirit be rather glorious? For if the ministration of condemnation be glory, much more doth the ministration of righteousness exceed in glory." Paul was teaching that the old system which condemned people had come to an end. Now there was a System working through the Grace of God within, which would unfold the divine heredity of perfection. "Seeing then that we have such hope, we use great plainness of speech: and not as Moses, which put a veil over his face, that the children of Israel could not steadfastly look to the end of that which is abolished; but their minds were blinded;

but until this day remaineth the same veil untaken away in the reading of the old testament; which veil is done away in Christ." With the veil of unillumination taken away Paul reminds us that "where the Spirit of the Lord is, there is liberty . . . we all, with open face beholding as in a glass the glory of the Lord, are changed into the *same image* from glory to glory." Such transformation comes from the Spirit of God unfolding from within. (II Cor. 3:9-18)

READ: Matt. 1:18-25; Matt., Chapter 2; Luke: Chapters 1 and 2.

CHAPTER IV

The Call and Preparation
for His Public Ministry

When the family returned to Nazareth, Joseph continued his work as a carpenter. He undoubtedly taught that trade to Jesus. Since Jesus was born into the Hebrew culture he was trained in the Jewish faith, and was well aware of the hundreds of written and oral observances that governed their daily lives.

The Gospels give us no insights into Jesus' childhood, with the exception of his 12th year, when he accompanied his parents to the Temple in Jerusalem for the Passover Feast. His family went with a caravan of other families. After the religious festivities, the caravan was proceeding back to Nazareth. They were a day's journey from Jerusalem when his parents realized that Jesus was missing. They returned to the Temple where they found him in the presence of the doctors of the law, the theologians. He was listening to what they had to say and asking them questions. Apparently he was responding too, for Luke tells us that "all that heard him were astonished at his understanding and answers." (Luke 2:47)

When his mother found him she naturally expressed her concern. She and Joseph had been looking for him everywhere and were probably very worried about him. Jesus asked his mother, "How is it that ye sought me? Wist ye not that I must be about my Father's business?" (Luke 2:49) His parents were unable to understand the deeper meaning of these words. Jesus had realized his oneness with God. While Mary did not have the spiritual understanding of his reply, she did treasure these sayings in her heart. (Luke 2:51)

One who was to be the forerunner of the Christ, and prepare the way for the Messiah, had been named by the ancient prophets. This one was John the Baptist who was just a few months older than Jesus. John's birth is also described as transcending the physical laws, but not in the same way as Jesus' birth. John's parents, Zacharias and Elizabeth, were elderly people, with Elizabeth well past child-bearing years.

They had in the past hoped and prayed for a child.

Zacharias was a priest. One day while he was praying in the Temple an angel appeared and told him that he and Elizabeth would have a child whose name was to be John. That this child was to have a greater expansion of consciousness than was demonstrated at that time is indicated in the angel's words: "He shall be filled with the Holy Ghost (Spirit) even from his mother's womb." (Luke 1:15) The angel added, "And he shall go before him (Jesus the Christ) in the spirit and power of Elias (Elijah), to turn the hearts of the fathers to the children, and the disobedient to the wisdom of the just; to make ready a people prepared for the Lord." (Luke 1:17)

Zacharias was unable to comprehend how it could be possible that he and his wife in their old age could have a child. His unbelief resulted in his being unable to speak until the day that John was born. The angel Gabriel, who brought Zacharias this message, and who told him that because of his unbelief he would be unable to speak, was the same messenger who announced to Mary that she would have a child.

When John was born and was to be named at the age of eight days, people were calling him Zacharias after his father. His mother said "Not so; but he shall be called John." Since there were no other family members named John, they insisted on trying to get his father to name him. His father asked for something on which to write. After he had written "His name is John," he was able to speak again. Zacharias later prophesied concerning his son: "Blessed be the Lord God of Israel; for he hath visited and redeemed his people. And hath raised up an horn of salvation for us in the house of his servant David; as he spake by the mouth of his holy prophets, which have been since the world began; that we should be saved from our enemies, and from the hand of all that hate us; to perform the mercy promised to our fathers, and to remember his holy covenant; the oath which he sware to our father Abraham, that he would grant unto us. That we being delivered out of the hand of our enemies might serve him without fear, in holiness and righteousness before him, all the days of our life. And

THE CALL AND PREPARATION FOR HIS PUBLIC MINISTRY

thou, child (John), shall be called the prophet of the Highest: for thou shalt go before the face of the Lord to prepare his ways; to give knowledge of salvation unto his people by the remission of their sins. Through the tender mercy of our God; whereby the dayspring from on high (Jesus) hath visited us; to give light to them that sit in darkness and in the shadow of death, to guide our feet into the way of peace." (Luke 1:57-79)

While we may not have any difficulty in realizing inherencies of God as mercy, kindness and forgiveness, Zacharias in stating these qualities was beyond the consciousness of the average Jew of his day. The religious leaders of that day had painted a picture of a God of judgment who needed to be constantly appeased with offerings and sacrifice.

Although Jesus and John were contemporaries, Luke gives no indication that they were ever together in their youth, despite the fact that their mothers were cousins. Two interesting contrasts are given regarding their youth. Luke's words concerning John are, "And the child grew, and waxed strong in spirit, and was in the deserts till the day of his shewing unto Israel." (Luke 1:80) (It is believed that John was a member of the Essenes.) Regarding Jesus, Luke writes, "And the child grew, and waxed strong in spirit, filled with wisdom: and the grace of God was upon him." (Luke 2:40)

The first 30 years of Jesus' life have sometimes been known as "the silent years," for aside from Luke's recording of the incident in the Temple, and other legends from the apocryphal writings, there are no written accounts. During those 30 years the creative activity of God was operative within him, preparing him for a three-year ministry that would revolutionize the world. We, too, may model our lives after the life of the Wayshower. We, too, can most effectively build the base for our spiritual undertakings by waiting patiently in the Silence in the Presence of God. There the parts may be seen in relation to the Whole. There the awareness of our oneness with the Father is evident, as we realize that "in him we live and move and have our being." We need not strive and strain, working with "might and power," but we rest in the flow of the Spirit and allow God to work through us. If we can be faithful to these silent times of waiting upon the Lord, He will manifest the Divine adjustments, the needed insights, and the perfect answers.

As John the Baptist was preparing for his call he realized that, unless mankind turned back to God, outer conditions would continue to deteriorate. John's whole focus, therefore, was on repentance—of having some remorse for following the ways of error. He realized that once he brought people to repentance, with a desire to go on in a deeper walk with God, he had nothing beyond the highest positive attributes of the Mosaic Law to give them. He knew that one was coming after him who was greater than he—the Messiah, the Deliverer, the Christ—and he stirred up a spirit of expectancy among his followers.

John was a very sincere man, but completely unsophisticated in his approach with people. One would not call him gentle. He called a "spade a spade," had very little tact, and as a result had many enemies, as well as friends and followers. John's were ethical teachings, beginning with, "Repent, for the Kingdom of Heaven is at hand." When a multitude of people came to him to be baptized, he insisted that they show some proof that they were worthy. When they asked what they should do he said, in essence, that they had better begin to *live* what they were giving lip service to. "He that hath two coats, let him impart to him that hath none, and he that hath meat, let him do likewise." (Luke 3:11) To the tax collectors he advised that they take no more from people than that to which they were entitled. To the soldiers he said, "Do violence to no man, neither accuse any falsely; and be content with your wages." (Luke 3:12-14) John was able to give ethical and moral advice to all walks of life. John himself lived the highest ethics through severe discipline. He asked no one to do what he had not done himself.

John's work culminated with baptizing his listeners with water (a symbol of purification) for the remission of sins. John's way was almost to frighten his hearers into repentance. Jesus' baptism was the baptism of the Holy Spirit within—the releasing of the Spirit to do the work of inner unfoldment.

One day while John was preaching and engendering expectation for the coming of the Christ, Jesus appeared. To get from Nazareth in Galilee to the Judean wilderness, where John was doing his work, was a long journey which would have taken days. When Jesus requested baptism and entered the Jordan River, John realized that here was one to whom the repentance message did not apply. He tried to stop Jesus by saying, "I have need to be baptized of thee, and comest thou to me?" Jesus replied that it should be so now, "for thus it becometh us to fulfill all righteousness." (Matt. 3:14-15)

Jesus met an important principle in this act. He identified at the level of those who were ready for his ministry. He found a common meeting place and he did not ask his followers to do anything that he would not do himself. The ancient prophets had noted this quality of meekness and humility in him as they said that he would be "reckoned with the transgressors." By spiritual law we shall always realize blessings through humble acts of love. Jesus opened his Sermon on the Mount with "Blessed are the poor in spirit (humble-minded) for theirs is the Kingdom of Heaven." (Matt. 5:1)

This act of love and humility brought Jesus to an overwhelming moment: "The heavens were opened unto him, and he saw the Spirit of God descending like a dove and lighting upon him; and lo, a voice from heaven, saying, This is my beloved Son, in whom I am well pleased." Up until the baptism, Jesus was no doubt *aware* of his identity. Just in that moment, though, The Father used the occasion to manifest in Jesus the full and permanent "charge" of God-*realization*—to cross suddenly and forever the line between knowing and *being*. That being the case, the moment may have filled both men with a nearly unbearable sweetness. How often are we privileged to look God in the face of one of our own?

While Jesus' way was not the way of John the Baptist, he nevertheless found a point of identification. He began his public ministry with John's teaching: "Repent, for the Kingdom of Heaven is at hand." Jesus saw the need to *begin* with a turning around, leaving states of error and duality, and focusing the attention upon God and His Kingdom. Jesus did not frighten or threaten his hearers. He simply said that it would be impossible to be divided—to serve "God and mammon," or Spirit and materiality. In order to build the inner treasure of the Kingdom and draw from its benefits, he urged a single-eyed approach.

Although Jesus identified with John's work, he was not condoning John's method of using "fear of the wrath to come"; nor was he condemning spiritual growth brought about by discipline and willpower as demonstrated by John. He was able to look within John's heart, and to know that his motives were pure. Jesus knew that John was a man utterly devoted to God, and he realized that John's work was necessary. We may not all follow the same path, or express in the same way, but it is important that we respect all sincere seekers of Truth if they are seeking God for Himself alone. John was the bridge—the highest that could be demonstrated under the Law—between the old dispensation and the Christ Way of Life.

Jesus summed up the contrast between the old and the new dispensations and made an evaluation of John the Baptist: "Among those that are born of women there is not a greater prophet than John the Baptist: but he that is least in the Kingdom of God is greater than he (John)." (Luke 7:28)

Following his baptism Jesus was led of the Spirit into the wilderness to be alone and ponder his ministry. There he met and overcame three soul tests—ones that we are dealing with constantly. These are the tests of avarice, greed for personal power, and *pride* or self-aggrandizement. The Israelites, forty years in the wilderness, did not master these tests. Jesus met and 'mastered them in forty days.

From his youth he had been filled with spiritual wisdom and understanding, and the Grace of God was working through him. The voice of temptation was now urging him to misuse his power—to elevate his own personality and to forget God's plans. These were actually the temptations of the race consciousness—urging the misuse of Divine energy. Jesus was a free agent, and at any time could have turned away from his Divinely appointed mission. We, too, have been given the same free will.

The first test came in the form of meeting a legitimate need when he was hungry. "Command these stones to become bread." Bread symbolizes the power of wealth, not only money, but name, fame, friends and prestige. We are tempted to use Spirit-substance to serve vested interests and promote ourselves. Jesus, realizing that he was already attuned to the wealth of the Kingdom of Heaven, answered "Man shall not live by bread alone, but by every word that proceedeth out of the mouth of God." (Matt. 4:4) The Word from the mouth of God is First Cause—that Divine activity that is the source of all "bread." He identified himself with the Reality of Spirit rather than the appearances of the world. He knew that his purpose was not to increase materiality and "lay up treasures on earth," but to build the "treasure within." Thus, in preparing for his ministry, he took his eyes off any personal gains and concentrated on the Will of God.

The second temptation was to cast himself down from the pinnacle of the temple, for "God shall give his angels charge concerning thee: and in their hands they shall bear thee up." (Matt 4:6) Inherent in this temptation was the prestige that he might gain if he publicly displayed this God-given power through all sorts of signs and wonders having no relevance to his Divine assignment. He chose not to impress people for these purposes, and answered with, "Thou shalt not tempt (misuse) the Lord thy God." (Matt. 4:7) To divert spiritual energy into the wrong channels can mean that one can "play with fire" and eventually be "burned." It cannot be used for negative purposes without suffering the consequences of the Law of Expression. We hear every day of the misuse of power for personal vested interests.

The third temptation had to do with the highest wall between us and God—the wall of pride. It sometimes is a subtle test, as are all three tests when we encounter them. Jesus was offered in this test "all the kingdoms of the world" if he would fall down and worship Satan (a state of mind that believes it can replace God or operate totally apart from God and His spiritual principles). "Satan" says, "You can do it on your own. Let your personality have full sway and leave God out of the picture." To this temptation Jesus answered, "Get thee hence, Satan: for it is written, Thou shalt worship the Lord thy God, and Him only shalt thou serve." Jesus put pride and self-aggrandizement out of the range of his spiritual vision. (Matt. 4:8-10)

Jesus mastered these tests and showed himself to be an intrinsically motivated Son of God. He revealed the Truth of God for its own sake and not for any personal gain or vested interests. In the end, he was willing to give his own life to serve the purposes of the Kingdom of God on earth.

A "wilderness" experience—a time of testing—seems to be required of every spiritual initiate. We have more than one such experience in our unfoldment. Such experiences serve to strengthen us—to reinforce Truth in our consciousness. As we move from one level of consciousness to another, we often may experience what Peter has called the "refiner's fire," as we drop all resistance to the Will of God in our lives.

These three tests—avarice, greed for power, and pride—deal with unhealthy ego states. The prophets of the Old Testament pointed to pride as the downfall of nations, and one of the greatest stumbling blocks to spiritual growth. The central issue is not how much power we can demonstrate, but how *transparent a vehicle we can become for the Christ to take over in us*. Jesus the Wayshower points out that the key to mastery over these tests lies in our awareness of our oneness with the Father, of our resting in the heart of Omnipresence, and allowing His Will to be done through us. When we abide in the perfection of that which Eternally IS, we shall know true peace and lasting joy. Jesus said that no one could take that from us. Paul said it is the peace which abides, that which surpasses human understanding.

READ: Matt. Chapter 3; Matt. 4:1-17; John 1:15-34

CHAPTER V

Messianic Concepts: His Initial Ministry in Galilee

Jesus remained faithful to his Father whom he recognized as Dependable Principle. He had to know the Presence of God in and through all his activities. He also had to know the Will of God and relate his entire ministry to that perfect Will.

It was very important that he not succumb to the Hebrew concept of the Messiah. For the Jews, who were accustomed to manipulating the externals of life in order to accomplish their goals, the Messiah (Christ) was viewed as the Anointed One, a national, charismatic leader, working for Israel only, and using military strategy if necessary to overcome their enemies. According to the ancient prophecies this Messiah would establish a kingdom, and the only kingdom they could conceive was an earthly one patterned after the Golden Era of Kings Saul, David and Solomon. The Messiah, they were convinced, would liberate the people, extend the national boundaries, and re-establish the throne of David.

Even John the Baptist, who had attained to the highest in consciousness under the Law, held to the Hebraic concept of the Messiah as a divinely appointed Deliverer who would restore the nation with justice and equity, working with the externals of life. He told his followers: "And now also the ax is laid unto the root of the trees: therefore every tree which bringeth not forth good fruit is hewn down, and cast into the fire. I indeed baptize you with water unto repentance; but he that cometh after me is mightier than I, whose shoes I am not worthy to bear; he shall baptize you with the Holy Ghost, and with fire: whose fan is in his hand, and he will thoroughly purge his floor, and gather his wheat into the garner; but he will burn up the chaff with unquenchable fire." (Matt 3:10-12)

Jesus' concept of the Messiah and his method of operation was so different that when John heard in prison about the works of Jesus he apparently became confused. John, therefore, sent some of his own disciples to ask Jesus, "Are you the one that should come, or do we look for another?" (Matt. 11:3)

Jesus knew his Messianic mission in Truth. The kingdom that he would establish would not be an earthly one. It would be a spiritual one, the Kingdom of God within the heart. The rule and reign of the love of God would be established "on earth as it is in heaven." It would entail trusting God for everything, and according to the degree of faith and trust, one could rest in the Truth that God is in charge of every detail of life—a constant, instant and abundant source of all that is.

Therefore, Jesus seldom referred to himself as the Messiah because of its Hebraic nationalistic connotations, although he made several acknowledgements that he was indeed the Christ, the anointed agent of God to usher in a new covenant, a new age. Most often he humbly referred to himself as Son of Man, a term used in the Book of Daniel, identifying with mankind in all ways, yet realizing that he was one with the Father and had been entrusted with establishing the Kingdom of God on earth.

After his baptism in the Jordan River by John the Baptist, Jesus was followed by two men who had been disciples of John. These two were to become his first disciples—Andrew and his brother, Simon Peter, both of whom were fishermen. Andrew recognized him as "the Messias, which is, being interpreted, the Christ." (John 1:41)

The next day, when Jesus was returning to Galilee, he found Philip and invited him to join their group. Philip in turn went to his friend, Nathaniel, and excitedly told him that they had found the One spoken of throughout their sacred writings, "him of whom Moses in the law, and the prophets, did write." (John 1:45)

In returning to his home province of Galilee, Jesus demonstrated an important principle in our walk in Truth. We need to deal with our immediate surroundings successfully and do our work there before leaping out to unknown vistas. There is a saying, "Bloom where you are planted," demonstrate the Truth in everyday life just where you are. This serves as a needed stepping stone to the next phase of soul unfoldment, for the Truth of God is built "line upon line, precept upon

41

precept"; and soul growth proceeds in divinely ordered stages.

When Jesus went to the synagogue in his own home town of Nazareth he read from the Book of Isaiah during the service of worship: "The Spirit of the Lord is upon me, because he hath appointed me to preach the gospel to the poor; he hath sent me to heal the broken-hearted, to preach deliverance to the captives, and recovering of sight to the blind, to set at liberty them that are bruised." (Luke 4:16-18, Isa. 61:1-3) When he acknowledged himself to be the fulfillment of that prophecy and mission, he became immediately unpopular. They looked upon him as merely the son of Joseph, one of the hometown boys. In fact, they became so angry that a neighborhood boy, a carpenter, would make such claims, that they drove him out of town with the intention of pushing him off the brow of the hill. However, he was able to know and demonstrate his complete protection. He walked straight through the whole crowd, protected by God's power.

Because those around us have free will, we are often unable to make any impression upon others until there is a state of receptivity—an openness to receive Truth. The Bible does not record, perhaps, the one or two sitting in the synagogue that day who may have been ready; nor does it follow through to show that Jesus planted a Divine Seed in the darkened consciousness, which in due time would make its impact. We must always leave results in God's hands when we receive the guidance and the Spirit-enablement to follow through on a spiritual task. We may never see visible results, but we may know that the work of Spirit continues in the invisible, and that Reality will manifest.

As he completed his work, Jesus moved on to the next appointed place. During his three-year ministry, the Gospels indicate that he made approximately 50 journeys. Some of these were of short duration; others much longer. Each ministering journey had a relationship to the whole of his work and he lost no time nor movement as he met each challenge presented to him in divine flow. He accompanied his teaching with "miraculous" demonstrations—these, too, following a sequential pattern of unfolding. First, he dealt with the *laws of matter*; transcending them to change water into wine (his first miracle), multiplying loaves and fishes, and commanding the elements of nature. Then he clarified the *laws of mind* (mental laws), as he taught his followers to make the right use of the work of thought. Finally, he opened their understanding of the *laws of Spirit*, showing that mind and matter were meant to serve Spirit. He demonstrated this in several instances when he raised the dead; and finally in the raising of Lazarus who had been dead in the tomb four days.

Jesus eventually called eight other disciples, making twelve in all. This little band made their headquarters in Capernaum in Galilee. As this Galilean ministry was established there came an end to the ministry of John the Baptist. He was eventually arrested by Herod Antipas and beheaded.

Jesus worked at all times from the Kingdom consciousness. For him it was all a matter of UNION with the Father. There was no attempt to strain to work his way into that Kingdom. He lived there always. "What I see the Father do, I do"—"What I hear the Father say, I say"—"I have come to do the Will of my Father." His divine goal and its implementation was stated in these words, revealing his relationship to the Father. This was his formula for Kingdom living. The Kingdom was *within* and manifested itself *without*. It was the work of this band of twelve to help him plant and nurture the Divine Seed within the hearts of the people, and then allow God's unfolding within them to bring forth the "blade, the ear, and the full corn," in divine order in the fullness of time. (Mark 4:26-28)

When Jesus taught at the synagogue in Capernaum, the people were "astonished at his doctrine for he taught them as one who had authority, and not as the scribes." (Mark 1:22) He was not only expanding their vision, but accompanying this with demonstrations of healings so that they asked, "What thing is this? What new doctrine is this?" (Mark 1:27) Jesus was later to tell his disciples concerning this new dispensation: "Blessed are the eyes which see the things that ye see: for I tell you, that many prophets and kings have desired to see those things which ye see, and have not seen them; and to hear those things which ye hear, and have not heard them." (Luke 10:23,24)

Jesus became so popular that when he visited a household there would be huge crowds who gathered, so great that the house could not hold them. Not all came because they were ready to apply his teachings. Many were there out of curiosity. Some came to spy upon him and report his activities to the local ecclesiastical authorities. Others came out of necessity. In one instance some friends of a man who had palsy were so anxious for his healing that when they could not enter the doorway of the house because of the crowd, they lowered him through the opening of the roof. Jesus was able to spiritually discern the inner cause of the inharmony that resulted in the sickness in those he healed, and he would "treat" for that impediment. In this man's case it was the result of sin, which could have been error of thought or action. Sin has its roots in denial of God and His ways—in lack of faith in God. "Whatever is not of faith (in God) is sin." (Rom. 14:23) There was absolutely no condemnation of this man—just a simple statement of fact concerning the cause of his illness, accompanied by the divine neutralizer, "Son, thy sins be forgiven thee." (Mark 2:5) The scribes were outraged that Jesus should assume such authority as forgiving sins. Only God could do this they reasoned. Jesus was quick to perceive false reasoning and backed up his words with the healing command, "Arise, and take up thy bed, and go thy way into thine house." (Mark 2:11) An instantaneous healing occurred. The man walked before this large gathering of people.

It was Jesus' custom to worship in the synagogue on the Sabbath day. On one such occasion he healed a man who had a "withered hand." He was immediately rebuked by the religious authorities for breaking the law of the Sabbath. He pointed out to them that their laws permitted them to rescue an animal that was in trouble on the Sabbath. How much more important it was to God that Man, His highest manifestation, should receive comfort and healing on the Sabbath. These Sabbath laws had not been made to bring their adherents into bondage, but rather to serve mankind. Jesus here teaches an important principle. In short, "institutions" are made by man to serve man, not the other way around. When we become in bondage to the "institution," and our lives begin to deteriorate because of it, it is time to make the necessary adjustments in order that life may flow in harmony with Spirit again. Mankind was never meant to live in limitation, however subtle, but to live in the consciousness of the Kingdom of Heaven.

Jesus was constantly being challenged by the religious authorities because his doctrine and his works were a radical departure from the status quo. He represented a real threat to their authority, for the crowds were gladly hearing him, following him wherever he went. When Jesus was in the home of Simon Peter, healing Peter's mother-in-law, "all the city was gathered together at the door." (Mark 1:33) In another house there was such a crowd gathered that "there was no room to receive them." (Mark 2:2) While the Twelve were a help to him, they had not reached that point in consciousness where they could adequately respond to the scribes, the lawyers, the Pharisees and Sadducees. Jesus was so established in the heart of the Father that the Father expressed through him to do the work. Because he was so *perfectly integrated with Spirit,* he was God in the *fullness of human activity and comprehension.* This is the reason that he could face this immobilized consciousness alone.

In order to get the groundwork completed in Galilee, he trained his Twelve and sent them out by twos with the message of the Kingdom of God, and with the authority to heal the sick. Symbolically, twelve stands for the number of completion. It also paralleled the twelve original tribes of Israel. He gave them some real practice in total reliance upon God as he instructed them, "Take nothing for your journey, neither staves, nor scrip, neither bread, neither money; neither have two coats apiece." (Luke 9:3) It is important for us to remember that Jesus always gave spiritual instruction on an INDIVIDUAL BASIS. He did not generalize one fixed set of instructions for all occasions. In this particular instance he had to quickly demonstrate to this band of twelve, who would carry on his work, that God is utterly dependable. There was not a great deal of time in which to get this concept fixed in their consciousness. Had he not been undergirding them in prayer, they could never have demonstrated what they did. On another occasion he sent out seventy disciples by twos, as he foresaw the need to speed up the work of sowing the seed of the Kingdom awareness in Galilee. Again he undergirded their work through his own established consciousness, and he had a vision of the spiritual impact of this work upon the race consciousness. He told them of this vision: "I beheld Satan as lightning fall from heaven." (Luke 10:18) The seventy disciples returned amazed that "even the devils (all forces of error and opposition to God) are subject to us through your name (your consciousness, your Being)." (Luke 10:17) Jesus extended their learning and indicated that they should not confine their rejoicing to watching outward demonstrations, but should center their rejoicing in the Truth that their names (the essence of their Beings) are established in Heaven. (Luke 10:20)

As Wayshower he tells us not to become enchanted by demonstrations per se, nor to allow our personalities to condescend to the spirit of pride (self-righteousness) in our spiritual accomplishments. Our vision must ever be fixed upon the Reality of God, the Source and Creator of all life . . . "of all things visible and invisible." The outer effects of life will follow in natural order if we place first things first and give God our total allegiance, trusting Him for everything. It is very easy to become "puffed up" with our own self-importance, to brand ourselves "special," to belittle the efforts of those who do not have "spiritual prominence." As the humble widow in complete faith cast her small "mite" into the temple treasury, Jesus was quick to say that her mite would serve God in a greater way than the large sums given for selfish motives. It is faithfulness to First Cause—God the Father—that gives us reason to rejoice and rest in Spirit.

Jesus was intrinsically motivated to serve Truth for the sake of Truth itself, not for what it could do for him. Unless all is surrendered to Spirit, he knew that the outer effects of these demonstrations would have little long-range value. He sought to bring forth Eternal values, Eternal profits, Eternal motives and released transient and temporary motives from his heart. This must be our Way, for our feet must ever follow his footsteps.

READ: Mark 1:14-45; Mark 3:1-10; Luke 4:14-44; Luke, Chapter 9; Luke, Chapter 10.

CHAPTER VI

His Galilean Ministry

As the Galilean ministry continued, the people pressed upon Jesus more and more for miracles. The focus of their attention was not upon seeking God for Himself and working cooperatively with Spirit, but upon the outer manifestations alone.

Jesus mentioned in particular three Galilean cities which had not been receptive to his message of the Kingdom of God on earth. These were Chorazin, Bethsaida and Capernaum. Capernaum, his headquarters, was unable to receive the message because of the opposition of pride. Jesus spoke of the city as exalting itself to heaven, and he prophesied that unless it turned to God it would be brought down. The three cities that Jesus mentioned were very prosperous, and this is the reason their inhabitants had difficulty with the Kingdom message. They relied upon materiality and found their security in their prosperity. Material wealth constitutes what the Bible calls "uncertain riches." Jesus said that it was easier for a camel (or "rope," according to Laamsa's translation) to go through the eye of a needle than for those whose hearts *trust* in riches to enter the Kingdom. And so it was with these Galilean cities.

Jesus was far from indifferent toward these cities. He loved the inhabitants enough to warn them that they would know suffering through the Law of Expression if they did not turn from the error of their ways and work cooperatively with Spirit. In his function as a prophet and Wayshower, he had to point out full effects of the Law of Expression, both positive and negative.

The purpose of Bible prophecy is not to spell inevitable doom that cannot be averted or changed. The purpose is to prevent individuals and groups from pursuing dangerous courses in life. The seer or prophet is able to envision future events—effects which are created by the individuals themselves—and makes every attempt to avoid calamity, to awaken the people to Truth and return them to Principle. The prophet does not condemn or pronounce judgment per se. The prophet merely relates the inevitable result of the Law of Expression, so that impending calamity may be avoided.

When Herod Antipas learned of Jesus' successes with the common people, he became very concerned and wanted to see him. Jesus was now a marked man, for Herod was determined to get rid of him. Some of the Pharisees told Jesus that he needed to leave or Herod would kill him. His answer to them was, "Go ye and tell that fox, Behold I cast out devils and I do cures today and tomorrow, and the third day I shall be perfected." (Luke 13:32) He was well aware of eventually giving his life and demonstrating the Resurrection on the third day after his death. His ministry would continue and would be finalized in victory despite any threats from Herod or the Jewish ecclesiastical powers.

As Jesus came to emphasize more and more the triumph of his death, his ministry was taking on a new focus. Despite the fact that there were successes with the Galilean ministry, and that he had the attention of the people, Jesus realized that their main interest was in his outward manifestations of spiritual power. They were quite content to remain complacent and allow him to do the work, rather than apply the principles he was teaching to their own lives. The Hebrew concept of the Messianic role remained evident, and Jesus also realized that it was possible that they would come and take him by force to make him a king. (John 6:15) This realization came to him after he had fed five thousand people by multiplying the loaves and fishes. (John 6:5-14)

So he withdrew from the people to be alone in communion with the Father. That evening his disciples got into a ship proceeding toward their headquarters in Capernaum. In the darkness of the night a storm arose at sea. As they were rowing they saw Jesus walking on the sea coming to the ship. They were very frightened until he spoke to them saying, "It is I; be not afraid." (John 6:20) After they had taken him aboard the ship they *immediately reached their destination* on the shore. Jesus was transcending the laws of matter, of time and of space. Matter, time and space are all earthly elements. Working from the Eternal Kingdom consciousness, Jesus was not subject to the limitations of earthly systems of measurement. (John 6:21)

On the next day, when people sought him, he told them that they were not seeking him because of himself alone, but because he was able to provide them with "loaves and fishes." He advised, "Labour not for the meat which perisheth, but for that meat which endureth unto everlasting life, which the Son of man shall give unto you; for him hath God the Father sealed." (John 6:27)

Mark records that "whithersoever he entered, into villages, or cities, or country, they laid the sick in the streets, and besought him that they might touch if it were but the border of his garment: and as many as touched him were made whole." (Mark 6:56) There is no indication that these crowds sought to learn the principles of the Kingdom from him; but rather that there was a *growing dependence upon him to do the work for them.*

As Wayshower, Jesus would not have us dependent upon an earthly teacher longer than is necessary. We must finally grow to discipline ourselves, apply spiritual principles, and prove all things for ourselves. Our spiritual work must be internalized— accepted from within and acted upon from within. We deter our soul journey as long as we look for another individual or group to do the work for us. No one can embrace the Creative Word of the Spirit of God for another. Likewise, good teachers recognize that their ultimate success is made manifest when they are no longer needed.

All spiritual leaders and teachers must be transparent vessels of God's Grace. Their effectiveness is determined by their degree of transparency. Their students should always be able to look through them and beyond them to the Father. Jesus said, "the Father that dwelleth in me, He doeth the works." (John 14:10) There is always the subtle attempt of the personality to insist on remaining important and special to other people, but as followers of Jesus we must relate his message of direct access to the Father through the Christ within us.

The Pharisees, too, were seeking "signs from heaven" from him. Outward displays of power, without a corresponding change in the consciousness of the people, would not serve the cause of the Kingdom. Over and over he received criticism from the Pharisees, because he and his disciples did not adhere to all the external observances of the Law. On one particular occasion the criticism was that Jesus' disciples were transgressing the "tradition of the elders," because they "wash not their hands when they eat bread." (Matt. 15:2) Jesus' response to them was not for the purpose of defending his ways, but an attempt to teach them Truth concerning the creative power and action of God. He referred them first to their own sacred writings. "Well hath Esaias prophesied . . . this people honoreth me with their lips but their heart is far from me . . . in vain do they worship me, teaching for doctrines the commandments of men. For laying aside the commandment of God, ye hold the tradition of men . . . Full well ye reject the commandment of God, (the workings of Love within) that ye may keep your own tradition . . . MAKING THE WORD (the creative power and activity) OF GOD of none effect through your tradition." (Mark 7:6-9, 13)

Jesus knew that if the creative Word of God could be activated *within the minds and hearts of mankind*, the limitations of earth's bondage would gradually be removed as the Spirit of God unfolded within them. He used this same occasion to call the people (during this encounter with the Pharisees) close to him so that they, too, could share in this primal lesson of Truth. "And when he had called all the people unto him, he said unto them, Hearken unto me every one of you, and understand: There is *nothing from without* a man, that *entering into him can defile him*; but the things which *come out of him, those are they that defile a man*. If any man have ears to hear, let him hear." (If you are spiritually ready to grasp this message, accept it into your consciousness and let it expand itself.) (Mark 7:14-16)

His immediate disciples had difficulty with this message, for up until then all rabbinical teaching and conditioning had centered itself on *self-improvement* through "the Law and the

Prophets," an *extrinsic* environment. Jesus' basic ministry served to expand the teaching of the *interior life* and the *inner journey in soul consciousness*. Thus he refined the lesson further to his Twelve. "Do ye not perceive, that whatsoever thing from without entereth into the man, it cannot defile him; because it entereth not into his heart (the subconscious and the soul) but into the belly, and goeth out into the draught, purging all meats? . . . for *from within, out of the heart of man*, proceed evil thoughts . . . . " (Mark 7:18-23) Jesus is describing manifestation as *proceeding from within*. He is teaching that *thought is creative*, that *mind must ever serve the cause of Spirit*, so that God Himself may be released within to do the work of perfection through us.

After this particular encounter with the Pharisees Jesus began his withdrawal from Galilee. He withdrew to "the borders of Tyre and Sidon, and entered into an house, and would have no man know it: but he could not be hid." (Mark 7:24) He was communing with the Father to receive direction as to the next phase of his ministry. At this time he was approached by a Greek woman from Syrophenicia. Her daughter apparently had a very serious mental and emotional disturbance—"My daughter is grievously vexed with a devil." (Matt. 15:22) Jesus' ministry up to this time had been with the house of Israel, but this marks the beginning of the new focus—the extension of his teaching to the Gentiles.

The groundwork that he laid in Galilee had its successes, but he longed for his listeners to apply his message to their own lives. This Gentile woman had not been trained in the basics of truth that were delivered to the Hebrews by Moses through the Law. Therefore, Jesus' teaching method with her (as it was with everyone) was on an *individual* basis. *He recognized individual needs and individual states of consciousness.* When she made her request for help *he was silent*. Some might infer that he was *indifferent*, but nothing could be further from the truth. He was assisting her with a work in consciousness, as well as her daughter. He wanted to stimulate her soul centers to draw from the wellsprings of faith. When he explained to her, "I am not sent but unto the lost sheep of the house of Israel," that fact did not discourage her at all. Her request was "Lord, help me" ... do this work for me. Jesus went on to indicate that Israel was first to receive his ministry, for "it is not meet to take the children's bread and to cast it to dogs." (Matt. 15:24-26) His meaning is, "Those who have been spiritually prepared (the house of Israel) receive the Kingdom first; and I would not impose spiritual activity upon those who do not, or are not ready to have an appreciation of the Gift of God." The word "dogs" was a term associated with the Gentiles at that time. We have experienced what happens when we "cast our pearls" of Truth before those who are not ready to receive them. This woman indicated, as Jesus was conditioning the soil of her consciousness, that she was ready and willing to cooperate with him in this healing of her daughter. "Truth Lord" (she agreed that the holy things of God should not be imposed upon people who would not appreciate them), "Yet the dogs eat of the crumbs which fall from their masters' table." Not only was her faith stimulated, but she was quick-witted. Jesus recognized her expansion in consciousness and realized that the work was done. He said to her "Woman, great is thy faith: be it unto thee even as thou wilt ... And her daughter was made whole from that very hour." (Matt. 15:27,28)

With this new focus of extending his work to the Gentiles, he also began to speak of his forthcoming suffering in order to give the necessary life and impetus to the rule and reign of the Kingdom of God on earth. "And he began to teach them that the Son of man must suffer many things, and be rejected of the elders, and of the chief priests, and scribes, and be killed, and after three days rise again." (Mark 8:27-31) From these happenings he said *the Kingdom would come with power*. "Verily I say unto you, That there be some of them that stand here, which shall not taste of death, *till they have seen the Kingdom of God come with power*." (Mark 9:1)

Of his twelve disciples Jesus had a small inner circle of three—Peter, James and John—to whom he imparted the deeper strata of teaching and spiritual experience. On one occasion, after Peter recognized him as the Christ, Jesus took the three into a high mountain to be alone with them. While there "he was transfigured before them, and his raiment became shining, exceeding white as snow . . . and there appeared unto them Elias (Elijah) and Moses: and they were talking with Jesus." (Mark 9:2-4) Here was a demonstration of transcendence over matter, time and space. Jesus brought Peter, James and John face to face with the Reality of dimensionless pure Spirit. Jesus, Elijah and Moses were conversing about the work of Jesus for earth. We gain some insights into the help for the affairs of men from the unseen world. Elisha once impressed this upon his fearful servant when they were surrounded by the Syrian armies. "Fear not," Elisha said, "for they that be with us are more than they that be with them." He prayed that his servant's eyes might be opened and the young man saw "the mountain was full of horses and chariots of fire round about Elisha." (2 Kings 6:16,17)

During this illumined experience, the conversation of Moses, Elijah and Jesus centered about the Master's death which would occur in Jerusalem. (Luke 9:30,31) Peter was so in awe of this experience that he suggested that they make three tabernacles, one for each personage. "There came a cloud, and overshadowed them and they feared as they entered in the cloud. And there came a voice out of the cloud, saying, This is my beloved Son; hear him. And when the voice was past, Jesus was found alone." (Luke 9:34-36; Mark 9:5-7) When they looked around they could no longer see Moses and Elijah, for these two leaders of Israel had been overshadowed. Only Jesus could be seen. Moses had stood for the highest from the Law, and Elijah had represented the highest in consciousness from the teachings of the prophets. God had shown Peter, James and John that these two were good—but what they were seeing in Jesus was the highest.

Even though Peter had previously acknowledged Jesus as the Christ, he did not have the understanding of the Christ. He was placing the best of the old dispensation of consciousness on an equal plane with the new. In moments of great illumination, it is a natural inclination to want to stay there, and not return to the valleys of service. The ongoing work of the Kingdom is done through us. We are God's hands and feet, the channels for his Truth and Love. If we try to keep the Experience for ourselves we will lose it altogether.

This Transfiguration experience was always a high point in Peter's life. He had probably dictated the account to Mark, and he also records it in his own epistle. (II Peter 1:17,18) Jesus had told Peter, James and John not to tell anyone of this experience until after he had risen from the dead. "And they kept that saying with themselves, questioning one with one another what the rising from the dead should mean." (Mark 9:10)

READ: Matt. 9:10-38; Mark, Chapter 7; Mark 9:1-10

CHAPTER VII

The Journey to Jerusalem

After Jesus had done all that was possible in Galilee (teaching and healing, and sending out the Twelve and Seventy to teach and heal), Luke records that "he steadfastly set his face to go to Jerusalem" to complete his final work. (Luke 9:51) "And he went through the cities and villages teaching and journeying toward Jerusalem." (Luke 13:22)

Peter did not like Jesus' telling them that completing the Messianic work would necessitate suffering. Peter probably felt that this would not be good for the group's morale, and he could not understand how the Deliverer could possibly open himself to suffering and death. Aside from Jesus' personal magnetism, the disciples were anxious to remain with him to watch him set up what they thought would be an earthly kingdom. With this earthly rule they were also contending for positions of power. Personal success and achievement at this point were very important to them. With the exception of John, they were all to scatter and leave Jesus alone when he came to face his greatest challenge, the Cross. Personal success and achievement is a subtle danger to soul growth, and this is why Jesus taught them that on the inner plane of being, the one who would be the greatest would become the servant of all. "Great" would be the ones who were seeking nothing for themselves, but sought only to *give of themselves for the sake of the Kingdom.*

Starr Daily has made an interesting summary of the basic world philosophies that have contributed to the unfoldment of the True Self. The ancient Greeks said, "Man, KNOW thyself"; understand your personality. The ancient Romans said, "Man, ORDER thyself"; discipline your personality. Buddha said, "Man, ANNIHILATE thyself"; become desireless, cut away the taproot of desire. Mohammed said, "Man, UNFOLD thyself," the unfolding process based upon obedience to the law of outer conduct. The Seven Fold Path of Yoga said, "Man, DEVELOP thyself." Jesus said, "Man, GIVE thyself"; love God with all your being and your neighbor as yourself.

The first five of these philosophies are primarily concerned with the *personality*, seeking to refine it, to bring it under control. They have all made a positive contribution to earth's consciousness. Jesus lifts this a step higher and says that, once you have controlled all this error that has entangled the personality and allowed Spirit to do this work of discipline and refinement, *then if you would be truly great ... empty yourself in LOVE to God and mankind*. This teaching of Jesus is based on an inherency of God. God is constantly giving Himself in the invisible and the visible world. He gives forth the Creative Substance out of which all has appeared for the blessing of His creation. When we make mistakes He forgives ("gives-for"). He "gives" of His own Divine Essence and neutralizes the error.

To clarify this important principle Jesus used a little child as an example of Godly action. He said that blessings would ensue if we were to give one little child a cup of water in his Name (consciousness). We would expect nothing in return from the little child in the form of external benefits (prestige, power, money, etc.). The only thing that a child could possibly give back to us is what the child might be holding in consciousness, the powerful intangibles of love and appreciation. Therefore, the real reward is *intrinsic*, not extrinsic. It comes from serving faithfully the advancement of the Christ Principle within us. "Whosoever shall receive one such child in my name receiveth me: and whosoever shall receive me receiveth not me but Him (God) that sent me." (Mark 9:37)

Peter had not yet reached that point in consciousness where he could release Jesus to walk into what he considered to be a death trap in Jerusalem. All the powers of Peter's conscious mind came to the fore. All those things which he could perceive through his outer sense, by way of the rational, deducting mind, came forth in an attempt to prevent Jesus from entering the city. Mark records the incident in this way: "And he began to teach them that the Son of man must suffer many things, and be rejected of the elders, and of the chief priests, and scribes, and be killed, and after three days rise again. And he spake that saying openly. And Peter took him, and began to rebuke him. But when he had turned about and looked on his disciples, he rebuked Peter, saying, Get thee behind me, Satan (adverse ego): for thou savourest not the things that be of God, but the things that be of men.''

"And when he had called the people unto him with his disciples also, he said unto them, Whosoever will come after me, let him deny himself, and take up his cross, and follow me." To deny oneself is to give up the demands of the unillumined personality. To "take up his cross" means to carry on with his soul learning and unfolding. "For whosoever will save his life (nurture the unillumined personality) shall lose it; but whosoever shall lose his life for my sake (the sake of the Christ) and the gospel's (the good news that proceeds from the realms of Spirit) shall save it (unfold God from within). For what shall it profit a man if he shall gain the whole world, and lose his own soul." (Mark 8:31-36)

The journey to Jerusalem took them through Samaria. The Jews had few dealings with the Samaritans and looked down upon them because they were "half-breeds"—Jew and Assyrian. The Samaritans, however, were also looking for the Messiah and had built their own temple on Mount Gerizim. On a previous visit to Samaria, Jesus had been welcomed and recognized as the Messiah, *after he had acknowledged that fact* to the woman at a well. On this returning journey, James and John, who went ahead possibly to obtain lodging for the group, were refused hospitality by the Samaritans. Because they were rejected, James and John wanted Jesus to channel power to them so that they could "command fire to come down from Heaven and consume them" (the Samaritans). James and John were infants and neophytes in the Spirit at this stage of their unfoldment. When they could not have their own way, they wanted to throw a spiritual "temper tantrum." This is the state that wants to use spiritual power in a negative way. When we are under extreme pressure, it is always a temptation to act in a negative way. Jesus immediately said, "Ye know not what manner of spirit ye are of. For the Son of man is not come to destroy men's lives, but to save them." (Luke 9:55,56)

Following this there are three valuable lessons of the Wayshower relative to earthbound ties that keep us from evolving. The first concerned a man who said that he would follow Jesus wherever he went. Jesus must have discerned that the man's motives for following Truth were some guarantees of earthly gain, of being able to settle down into a comfort zone and letting Jesus do his growing for him. Jesus could not give this kind of assurance, for he said, "Foxes have holes, and birds of the air have nests, but the Son of man hath not where to lay his head." (Luke 9:58) Living in the Kingdom will give us all the supply that we need, but it will not permit us to halt the growth process. We must go on expanding. If we seek it only for supply, we shall not know its full benefits.

Jesus was aware that another man was on the verge of being ready, for he issued him an invitation to join them as he said, "Follow me." The man was willing but said, "Lord, suffer me first to go and bury my father." Jesus said, "Let the dead bury their dead: but go thou and preach the Kingdom of God." (Luke 9:59,60) One thing was holding this man from his soul progression—a spiritual thief of the past, which urged him to hold on to some old hurt or resentment or some cherished earthly belief. Jesus the Wayshower tells us that *the past is dead—* it has *no power over us except what we wish to give it*. Those who live in the past must take care of the past—the dead past must bury its own dead. In states of unillumination we live either in the past or in the fear of the future; but when we live in the Kingdom there is only the Eternal NOW, from which all outer events flow in perfect order and perfect sequence under the instant, constant and abiding Presence of God.

A third aspirant to the Kingdom way of life asked if he could go with Jesus, but requested that he "first go bid them farewell, which are at home at my house." Jesus said to him "No man, having put his hand to the plow, and looking back, is fit for the Kingdom of God." (Luke 9:61,62) We will always find excuses for not carrying through with spiritual principles NOW. The old level of awareness makes its demands upon us and insists on our giving it one last look; but once we have decided to follow Jesus (the Wayshower of Truth) we cannot return to give these lesser realities our attention and commitment. Success in prayer, meditation, and spiritual work means that we leave these "problems" on the outside, and go within that inner chamber of the soul stripped of them— waiting in the Presence of God, and knowing that He is actively adjusting every detail of our lives and the lives of others. It is to this that we must give our thought and full attention. Appearances have no power in the Presence of the One and only Reality.

Another valuable spiritual lesson is to be learned from a rich young ruler who apparently had done his best at keeping the Mosaic Law. He asked, "Good Master, what shall I do that I may inherit eternal life?" Jesus immediately discerned that this young man looked at the externals of life and considered solely the personality. Jesus said to him, "Why callest thou me (your earthly idea of me) good? There is none good but one, that is, God." Jesus' desire was that mankind could recognize his work as the *activity of God expressing through him*. He did not want his own personality to receive the credit. As their conversation continued, the young man indicated to Jesus that he knew well the commandments. "Master, all these have I observed from my youth." "Then Jesus beholding him LOVED him, and said unto him, One thing thou lackest: go thy way, sell whatsoever thou hast, and give to the poor, and thou shalt have treasure in Heaven: and come, take up the cross, and follow me." (Mark 10:18-21) *Jesus again prescribed on an individual basis to meet an individual need*. He did not tell all the wealthy people who followed him to sell all that they had; but he saw this person, with good intent, having *his sole source of security in materiality*. His wealth and possessions were standing in the way at this point in his soul unfoldment. The story goes on to say that the young man went away grieved, for he had great possessions. He was still subject to all the good of the Old Covenant, but he was unable to grasp the Kingdom Idea, because his trust was not in God but in his great wealth. One of the foundation principles of living in the Kingdom is *trusting God for everything*.

We see this corporate lesson of consciousness in activity now. People are looking to the outer, attempting to manipulate and overpower the externals of life in order to have security. Perhaps we are being "pushed to the wall" with the pictures of inadequate retirement needs, energy and food shortages, world peace issues, and a host of other human requirements, coming to an all-time climax. These problems appear insurmountable, but they may turn out to be a lesson in Divine Awareness, for we shall have to let go of them and let God take over and care for us. Jesus asked in his Sermon on the Mount "Which of you by taking thought" (worrying and striving) can change an outer condition? "If God so clothe the grass of the field, which today is, and tomorrow is cast into the oven, shall He not much more clothe you, O ye of little faith? Therefore take no thought, saying, What shall we eat? or, What shall we drink? or, Wherewithal shall we be clothed? . . . But *seek ye first the Kingdom of God, and His righteousness; and all these things shall be added unto you*." (Matt. 6:27, 30, 31, 33)

As Jesus and his band of followers neared Jerusalem, they came to Jericho, within 17 miles of the city. They began to register fear on the one hand and excitement on the other, for the people were expecting that this earthly, external Kingdom of God would suddenly appear that very hour. (Luke 19:11) Jesus sought to lead them to true understanding by relating parables about the Kingdom. The parable was his teaching method to the crowds—a simple story that had to do with everyday occurrences within their culture. Jesus advocated *simplicity* of life and of teaching; and in these parables were great and profound truths. The parable had within it the properties of expansion so that the learner could first glean from its outer shell, then uncover deeper and deeper mysteries as the learning proceeded with a commensurate development of consciousness.

Throughout these parables Jesus presented a picture of the Kingdom quite different from what the people excitedly expected. In this teaching method he let them know that he would not be staying with them to rule on earth in the physical sense; that the Kingdom would not come into full manifestation at that very hour, as they were expecting that it should; but that they could expect to see it manifested in power after his death. The Book of the Acts of the Apostles relates many incidents about the power of the Kingdom in outer activity.

For those who would accept the rule and reign of God within their hearts, there would be the possibility of reaping one-hundred fold from the Kingdom treasures; but for those who chose to set their attention and allegiance upon the externals of life, there would be a soul dormancy and an inability to flow in harmony with God activity.

As Jesus viewed everything from the domain of Spirit he was able to perceive the disintegration of the old concept of Jerusalem, and the coming into awareness of the New Jerusalem—the Spiritual City—the inner habitation of peace, pressing through to earth's consciousness in a concentrated spiritual momentum.

READ: Matt. 18; Mark 10:17-52; Luke 15; John 4:5-42

CHAPTER VIII

Transcending the Law

The first phase of Jesus' ministry was his work in Galilee. The second phase began after his withdrawal from Galilee, as he ministered to places along the way on his journey to Jerusalem. The third phase began when he arrived in Jerusalem, the location of the beloved Temple, and the center of their religious life.

Jesus came to Jerusalem by way of Bethphage and Bethany. The meaning of the word Bethphage means "house of unripened figs." Jesus taught a parable about the vineyard of figs, which symbolized Israel. The parable pointed out that since Israel had failed in transmitting God-consciousness to the world, the vineyard was to be taken from her and given to others, so that the unfoldment process could proceed. The Gentiles would take up the cause. The fig tree which withered and died represented the unillumined consciousness that was unable to feed the life of Spirit to the world.

In this great religious center of Jerusalem Jesus was continuously confronted with the scribes, the lawyers, the Pharisees and the Sadducees. Since Jesus had the consciousness to back up all his teaching with visible demonstrations, he posed a real threat to the Jewish religious establishment. He was gaining great influence with the crowds. The religious leaders had, up to this point, kept the people in spiritual bondage. Jesus had said that the lawyers had taken away the key of knowledge. The leaders were mainly interested in their own self-preservation and had taken advantage of their positions of leadership in many ways. They quickly condemned and judged anything which they did not understand.

A few of the Pharisees were able to make a great leap in consciousness and profit from Jesus' work. Nicodemus and Joseph of Arimathea were two who became followers of the Master. However, for the most part, the religious leaders put every kind of stumbling block in Jesus' way. They often asked him by what authority he did his work. What were his credentials? They also attempted to trap him into arguments.

Because Jesus was attuned completely to the Father, he was able to avoid such traps and outwit all those who sought to entangle him.

The Pharisees sought to bind eternal guilt upon those whom they felt did not keep the letter of the Law. Jesus was quick to release people from such feelings of guilt in every instance that he encountered. One example is of the woman taken in adultery—as the Pharisees had reported "taken in the very act." (John 8:4) They appear not only to have openly condemned this woman, but must have gone out of their way to seek out any behavior which appeared to deviate from the "accepted" standard of the Law.

Having witnessed this act, they were anxious to see that she paid the death penalty, as prescribed in the minutia of detail that had become "the Law." They showed no compassion for the offender, and no consideration of rehabilitation. They even made their own exceptions to the Law, for under it *both* parties were to be brought "unto the gate of the city and ye shall stone them with stones until they die." (Deut. 22:24) They excluded the man in this case, carrying out their dual standard. Women at that time were considered chattels and second-class citizens. One of the great impacts of Jesus' life is that he immediately raised the status of women! The inconsistencies of the scribes and Pharisees, as well as their unillumined consciousness, caused Jesus to call them blind leaders of the blind.

While they were determined to make this woman suffer, this was not their primary reason for presenting her to Jesus. They were laying a subtle trap to see if he would follow the Mosaic Law in this case. If he advocated that she be stoned, this would undoubtedly cause a riot outside the city gates and upset the Roman authorities. Jesus would have been accused of insurrection. Rome was willing for the Jews to go through the motions of religious practice, as long as there was no occurrence that might incite a riot. But if Jesus did not advocate stoning, then he would appear to condone this woman's behavior, thereby disregarding the Law. Either way, the Pharisees reasoned that he would be in trouble.

Jesus did not reside in the world of duality where one decision is pitted against another, with neither centered in Truth and Righteousness. He rose above the pairs of opposites because his consciousness rested in the Father, where the perfect answer and perfect guidance reside. He applied a principle which transcended the Law of Moses, emanating from the purity of Spirit. It did not condone sinful acts, but neither did he condemn the offender. This all-encompassing principle went even further, for it did not leave the person involved in a state of spiritual lethargy. Jesus' treatment was to prime the wellsprings of this woman's soul and reach the cause of the deviancy, make the needed spiritual adjustment, and set her free.

It is recorded that Jesus stooped down and wrote with his finger on the ground. What he wrote the Gospelers do not tell us, but the words were such that these uncompassionate accusers shrank away from their verbal judgments and were forced to look at themselves. It is possible that he communicated some of his teaching from the Sermon on the Mount, which was applicable to this case . . . "Ye have heard that it was said by them of old time, Thou shalt not commit adultery: But I say unto you that whosoever looketh on a woman to lust after her hath committed adultery with her already in his heart." (Matt. 5:27,28)

Jesus actually ignored their accusations. He did not entangle himself with them. It was as though he did not hear them. Instead he said, "He that is without sin among you, let him first cast a stone at her. And again he stooped down, and wrote on the ground. And they which heard it, being convicted by their own conscience, went out one by one, beginning at the eldest, even unto the last: and Jesus was left alone, and the woman standing in the midst." (John 8:7-9)

Now this woman who had been so frightened stood alone in the Perfection of the Christ. The fear left her, for the power of his compassion revealed one who truly cared for her and loved her. He was showing her how to seek love on a higher level than she had previously known. "When Jesus had lifted up himself (from writing on the ground), and saw none but the woman, he said unto her, Woman, where are those thine accusers? hath no man condemned thee? She said, No man, Lord. And Jesus said, Neither do I condemn thee: go, and sin no more." (John 8:10,11)

When Jesus said "Neither do I condemn thee" he had brought to the word level the power of Spirit to neutralize the error of the past in her life. He had assured her that the mistakes of the past need not thwart the creativity of the present or the future. This was the first part of his treatment for her. He released her completely from the bondage of the past. The second part of the spiritual treatment—"Go, and sin no more"—was telling her not to misuse her free will by directing her creative energies into negative channels. Jesus' spiritual treatment did not destroy her innate dignity; rather, he strengthened her spirit.

As Jesus' popularity and success continued in Jerusalem, he could have been tempted to turn his attention to the prestige he was receiving. The Pharisees had said, "The world is gone after him." (John 12:19) Jesus manifested the inherency of wisdom. He realized that he could never commit himself to people, because popular opinion can be for us one day and against us another day. At best it is a transitory blessing. The Apostle John said "He (Jesus) knew all men." (John 2:24) Jesus well understood human nature, and that is why he always placed his trust in God—in Dependable Principle—rather than in people.

At the height of his popularity the chief priests, scribes and elders would have seized him, but they were fearful because the crowds were caught up with him. They feared that if they made any attempts to harm him there would be a public reaction that might backfire and get them in trouble with the Roman authorities. So they continued to undermine his work, trying to find some loophole whereby they might build up a case against him as a transgressor against the Mosaic Law.

One of the scribes, who was sincerely interested in

understanding the deeper meaning of the Ten Commandments, asked Jesus which was the first or the greatest commandment of all. Jesus replied, "The first of all the commandments is, Hear, O Israel; the Lord our God is one Lord: And thou shalt love the Lord thy God with all thy heart, and with all thy soul, and with all thy mind, and with all thy strength: this is the first commandment. And the second is like, namely this, Thou shalt love thy neighbour as thyself. There is none other command- ment greater than these." (Mark 12:28-31) The scribe immediately gained spiritual insight into far-reaching effects of this great teaching, and he said that this transcended "all the whole burnt offerings and sacrifices." "And when Jesus saw that he answered discreetly (with spiritual understanding), he said unto him, Thou art not far from the Kingdom of God." (Mark 12:33,34) Jesus was praising him for being able to get beyond the belief in the necessity of appeasing God through burnt offerings and sacrifices—the current practice of Judaism at that time. This scribe had made a giant leap in consciousness, to be able to accept Jesus' Summary of the Law. But then, to go on to discern spiritually the key to Life and direct access to God, propelled him a step further. Now Jesus was challenging him to make the next leap in consciousness and *apply that understanding to living.* Until we apply the teaching we can be said to be "not far" from awareness of the Kingdom, but to truly *experience*, we must make practical application of spiritual principles to daily living. To know about a Truth intellectually is one thing; to bring that Truth to the level of application is to appropriate its essence. To live and experience Life from that standpoint is Reality. We are called upon not only to know Truth, but to apply the principles, to *live* Truth.

Living life from the Kingdom consciousness brings about a *multiplication process of good*—an ever-expanding, creative flow of invisible Substance into the manifested creation. Jesus demonstrated this with matter, in multiplying the loaves and fishes. He pointed out that the humble widow's mite would multiply itself to serve the work of God in a great way. Working cooperatively with Spirit, we tap the Fount of Living Water, and the multiplication process begins to meet our every need, both tangible and intangible. When the disciples needed money to pay their taxes (tribute money), Jesus was able to demonstrate this multiplication process again by having Peter catch a fish with a coin in its mouth adequate to meet the taxation requirement. (Matt. 17:25-27)

While Jesus had success in assisting many to glimpse the depth of his teaching of this inward journey in consciousness, the Kingdom's message was not being received at the heart of Judaism. He realized the next major step would be giving up his life (his final impact upon the race consciousness) as a holy, living experiment, so that from that sacrificial act of love could come *the primal seed of the expansion of the multiplying process.* He was later to say concerning his death, "The hour is come, that the Son of man should be glorified. Verily, verily, I say unto you, Except a corn of wheat fall into the ground and die, it abideth alone; but if it die, it bringeth forth much fruit." (John 12:23,24) Jesus also indicated, as far as his death was concerned, " . . . I lay down my life, that I might take it again. No man taketh it from me, but I lay it down of myself. I have power to lay it down, and I have power to take it again. This commandment have I received of my Father." (John 10:17,18)

Jesus' teachings divided many among the Jews. Some considered him mad or insane. Others felt that his teachings and miracles had validity. Finally, at a winter dedication festival in Jerusalem, "came the Jews round about him, and said unto him, How long dost thou make us to doubt? If thou be the Christ, tell us plainly. Jesus answered them, I told you, and ye believed not: the works that I do in my Father's Name, they bear witness of me. But ye believe not, because ye are not of my sheep, as I said unto you. My sheep hear my voice, and I know them, and they follow me: And I give unto them Eternal Life; and they shall never perish, neither shall any man pluck them out of my hand. My Father, which gave them me, is greater than all; and no man is able to pluck them out of my Father's hand. I and my Father are one." (John 10:22-30)

At this they took up stones to stone him. Jesus asked, For which of his works and demonstrations did they wish to stone him? They answered, "For a good work we stone thee not; but for *blasphemy*; and because that thou, *being a man, makest thyself God.* Jesus answered them, Is it not written in your law, I said, Ye are gods? If he called them gods, unto whom the Word of God came, and the scripture cannot be broken; say ye of him whom the Father hath sanctified and sent into the world, Thou blasphemest; because I said I am the Son of God? If I do not the works of my Father, believe me not. But if I do, though ye believe not me, believe the works: that ye may know, and believe, that the Father is in me, and I in him." (John 10:31-38)

In declaring his own divinity, Jesus was also pointing out in their scripture, "Ye are gods" (Psalm 82:6), the *dormant divinity which lay within them.* The difference between them, he is saying, is that he is not only aware of his Divine nature, but his total being has been consecrated and perfected by the Father. As the Christ he was Perfected Son of the Father in human expression.

Their attempts to seize him were not successful. He was able to elude them. According to many scholars he had been in Jerusalem about three months, and now he would spend another three months away from Jerusalem in a town called Ephraim near the wilderness. (John 11:54) His disciples went with him. He was to make a spiritual preparation in consciousness for what, to the world, would spell failure, but to the Spirit would mean triumph and success.

Before he left Jerusalem for Ephraim he wept over the city, for he loved it and its inhabitants. Prophetically, he knew that it was going to meet with destruction (which it did in 70 A.D.) unless it would turn back to God. He would now be away from the city for some time. While he was in Ephraim there would be no more daily teaching in the Temple . . . no more of his going out at night and spending time on the Mount of Olives in prayer . . . for he had completed all that was possible in that city. He left it in tears. "O Jerusalem, Jerusalem, which killest the prophets, and stonest them that are sent unto thee; how often would I have gathered thy children together, as a hen doth gather her brood under her wings, and ye would not! Behold, your house is left unto you desolate: and verily I say unto you, Ye shall not see me, until the time come when ye shall say, Blessed is he that cometh in the name of the Lord." (Luke 13:34,35)

In the same wilderness where Ephraim was located, Jesus had met his first temptations right after his baptism by John the Baptist. Being aware of all that human personality can feel, surely he must have been tempted again to misuse his power to interfere with the Law of Expression for Jerusalem—to make some great show of power to make the people really "sit up and take notice." Foreseeing all that awaited him through Gethsemane and the Cross, he must have been tempted to walk away from it. But he knew the importance of taking this time to withdraw, and stay in the flow of the Father's Light and Love, so that he might appropriate all that was necessary from the Father's Life to bring his God-appointed mission to perfection. He demonstrated soul mastery over any and all subtle temptations. "We have not an high priest which cannot be touched with the feeling of our infirmities; but was in all points tempted like as we are, yet without sin" (without succumbing to error and limitation). (Heb. 4:15) He stayed in harmony with Heaven's plan for earth, judging "not according to the appearance, but . . . righteous judgment." (John 7:24)

READ: Mark 12:13-27; John 5:30-47; John 8:25-32

CHAPTER IX

His Mystical Teaching

Before he returned to Jerusalem from the wilderness town of Ephraim, Jesus received word that one of his close friends, Lazarus (the brother of Mary and Martha) was very ill and not expected to live. The sisters sent word for Jesus, hoping that he would come to give them some assistance. Jesus did something distinctly out of character. *He stayed away.* He said to his disciples, "This sickness is not unto death, but for the glory of God, that the Son of God might be glorified thereby." (John 11:4) He was inferring that a higher purpose, a greater demonstration of God-Power would later come.

He stayed in Perea for two days and then said to his disciples, "Let us go into Judea again." His disciples were very concerned, and they reminded him: "Master, the Jews of late sought to stone thee, and goest thou thither again?" (John 11:7-8) Jesus indicated to them that it was important to follow through on Divine guidance, to walk in the light of that guidance. He went on to tell them, "Our friend Lazarus sleepeth; but I go, that I may awake him out of sleep." His disciples could see no reason for Jesus to risk his life just to awaken someone from sleep. So Jesus had to tell them plainly, *"Lazarus is dead.* And I am glad for your sakes that I was not there, to the intent ye may believe; nevertheless let us go unto him." (John 11:11-15)

Upon their arrival in Bethany, Lazarus had been dead and in the grave (tomb) four days. Mary and Martha were receiving sympathy from their friends over their brother's death. "Then Martha, as soon as she heard that Jesus was coming, went and met him: but Mary sat still in the house. Then said Martha unto Jesus, Lord, if thou hadst been here, my brother had not died. But I know, that even now, whatsoever thou wilt ask of God, God will give it thee. Jesus saith unto her, Thy brother shall rise again. Martha saith unto him I know that he shall rise again in the resurrection at the last day. Jesus said unto her, I am the resurrection, and the life; he that believeth in me, though he were dead, yet shall he live; and whosoever liveth and believeth in me shall never die. Believest thou this? She saith unto him, Yea, Lord: I believe that thou art the Christ, the Son of God, which should come into the world." (John 11:19-27) Martha then called her sister Mary to let her know: "The Master is come and calleth for thee."

Mary also told Jesus that she believed that had he been there Lazarus would not have died. Both the sisters had the faith to believe that Jesus could have healed him. They were very good friends of Jesus and he had been in their home on many occasions. They undoubtedly had witnessed many of his miracles of healing.

Jesus asked to be taken to the grave. Lazarus had been buried in a cave (or tomb), and a stone had been placed before the door of it. When Jesus asked that the stone be removed Martha was very upset, reminding Jesus that Lazarus' body after being buried *four days* would have begun to decay and "by this time he stinketh." The Master desired that she trust him. Jesus insisted that the stone be removed, and after an audible prayer to the Father, "he cried with a loud voice, Lazarus, come forth.And he that was dead came forth, bound hand and foot with grave clothes; and his face was bound about with a napkin. Jesus saith unto them, Loose him, and let him go." (John 11:39-44)

This supreme "miracle" was to have varying repercussions. Many of the Jews who had been there to comfort Mary and Martha now believed in Jesus. Others went immediately to the Pharisees to report what had happened. Jesus knew that this tremendous demonstration signed his own death warrant.

Jesus had reasons for waiting until Lazarus had died before offering assistance. First, he attempted to teach his disciples the truth about death—"our friend. . . sleepeth." Death is not a finality, but a changed state of consciousness. Second, he wanted to demonstrate the supremacy of Spirit over matter. Third, he wanted to prove his power to resurrect the dead and present a preview of his own resurrection. By performing this "miracle," and by going through death himself, it would be possible for him to "deliver them who through fear of death were all their lifetime subject to bondage." (Heb. 2:15) Death to the Jews of that time meant a lesser existence than they were experiencing in life on earth.

After this, the Pharisees and the chief priests met in a council and decided that they had to do something about Jesus. If he were allowed to continue with these supernatural demonstrations, they concluded that everyone was going to be following him; and there would eventually be problems with the Romans as the excitement over him mounted. More enthusiasm over the Messianic movement would represent a real threat to the Romans in authority at that time. Then, too, these high priestly groups were reaping huge revenues from the Temple, and they did not want anything to happen that would upset their vested interests. Actually Rome was very indifferent about the Hebrew faith as long as it did not pose a threat to the Empire's aspirations or incite riots among the people. However, it would not take much to stir up the Zealots, the Jewish patriots, to start an insurrection movement; and if they thought the Messiah was behind them that would only serve to fan the flames.

Any way they looked at it, the chief priests and the Pharisees could see they had to get rid of Jesus. Caiaphas, the high priest that year, lost no time in getting the process started. An order went out from the religious council that if anyone knew the whereabouts of Jesus, it was to be reported.

Since the raising of Lazarus, Jesus could not walk "openly among the Jews," so he went back into the wilderness with his disciples. It becomes quite difficult to pinpoint the chronology of events at this time. From John's record it appears that Jesus came from Perea to Bethany where he raised Lazarus from the dead and then returned to Ephraim in the wilderness area.

Six days before the Feast of the Passover Jesus returned to Jerusalem. This would have been in early spring. As soon as the chief priests learned that he had returned, they were all for *seeking out Lazarus* and *putting him to death, too,* since the "miracle" of raising him from the dead had caused so many people to follow Jesus. The *crowds* were with Jesus, *as well as his disciples.*

He came into the city riding a borrowed donkey (symbol of humility) and the throngs which followed him expected that the Messiah had come to restore the kingdom of David. They expected him to start a great political revival and restore Israel's former glory, likened to King David's reign. Jesus came into the city riding this donkey (a quiet animal) because he wished to dramatize himself in a different role. He used every means of teaching to get his lessons across. He did not ride a war horse as a pompous king or general. He had come to the city for peace, not insurrection and war. He had no intention of using might and force in order to liberate the Jews. He had come to lead them to freedom from *within*, and this inner peace and freedom would transcend all the external conditions that were so grievous to them. Through his quiet, silent communion with the Father, Jesus tuned in to His Omniscient Power; and he longed to teach the people how to make this contact for themselves.

His enthusiastic followers spread their garments in the way and cut down branches from the trees, laying them in a path before him. They heralded him with shouts of, "Blessed is he that cometh in the name of the Lord: Blessed be the kingdom of our father David, that cometh in the name of the Lord: Hosanna in the highest." (Mark 11:9-10)

Mark tells us that Jesus went into the Temple and observed what was going on there. He said nothing but went out and retired that evening in Bethany, probably at the home of Mary, Martha and Lazarus.

When he returned to the Temple the next day he took action against the illicit business enterprises that were going on there. John's Gospel records that Jesus made a whip of small cords. He did not use it on people, as some have thought. Jesus did not advocate violence, *nor did he use violence in this instance.* The whip was used to *direct* all the cattle out of the

Temple, "oxen and sheep." This was a sudden, abrupt outer cleansing of the House of God. He would not waste his substance on argument and persuasion that this should be done. He knew that that kind of activity would get him nowhere. He simply acted, and acted immediately. Dumping the exchange tables and driving out the cattle and sacrificial doves was not an act of violence, however. This was the accepted manner of directing the movement of animals. The true worshipper, Jesus knew, must accept true religion as inherently the greatest of all realities. True religion is the acknowledgment of the only Reality—God, the All in All. The current temple worship was causing religion to become a means of commercialized profit-making. Not only did these interests degrade the purpose of the Temple (prayer)—but the noise of the oxen and sheep and the other animals, as well as the smell, hardly helped condition the consciousness of prayer. "And he taught, saying unto them, Is it not written, My house shall be called of all nations the house of prayer? but ye have made it a den of thieves." (Mark 11:15-17)

There was another reason for Jesus driving the traders out of the Temple. This Court of the Gentiles (part of the Temple itself) provided access to anyone—Jew or Gentile. To allow this part to become a commercial marketplace was to give the image of limitation upon the universal quality of God's Being— a denial of Omnipresence. The office of the Messiah must proclaim God's love for *all* people, as well as His Universal Presence, active and sacred at all times and in all places. Thus, the activities of the Temple were a violation of Truth, a distortion of the nature of God. The inscription between the court of the Temple and the inner court graphically recorded the error of sectarianism and exclusiveness. It read, "No stranger is to enter the balustrade. Whoever is caught will be answerable for his death which will ensue." Thus Jesus said to those who were selling doves, "Take these things hence; make not my Father's house an house of merchandise." (John 2:16) "My house shall be called *of all nations* the house of prayer." (Mark 11:17)

Not only were many of the Jewish people following him,

but there were some Gentiles as well. Some Greeks who had come to the city to partake in the Festival came to Philip, one of Jesus' twelve disciples, and requested to see the Master. When Philip and Andrew, another disciple, told Jesus about this, instead of rushing out to pick up more followers he told his disciples again that the time had come for his suffering. "Now is my soul troubled: and what shall I say? Father, save me from this hour: but for this cause came I unto this hour. Father, glorify thy name. Then came there a voice from heaven, saying, I have both glorified it, and will glorify it again." (John 12:27-28)

Jesus told them that this clairaudient illumination had come for their sakes and not for his. These supernatural experiences by way of voices, visions of Moses and Elijah, the transfiguration of the Christ, in addition to the "miracles" which they witnessed, were all given to assist their awareness that they were in the Mind of the Father, receiving their Life and Substance from Him. There was communication between earth and the Life of the Spirit. The great prophets prior to Jesus had dreamed dreams—they had had visions of what the earth would be like when it was flowing in Divine Harmony. The Prophet Habakkuk was among those who said, "for the earth shall be filled with the KNOWLEDGE of the glory of the Lord as the waters cover the sea." (Hab. 2:14) These seers realized that God's glory was already here—that we have always had it. In it "we live and move and have our being" (Acts 17:28), but earth had lost its *awareness* of this Truth. It was as if divinity lay dormant in the heart of the earth; and the spiritual work through the consciousness of Jesus was to activate it to bring mankind back into the consciousness of oneness with God.

Jesus did much to activate and condition the consciousness around him by words and acts of Truth. Because there was a failure on the part of the people to arrive at the application stage of his teaching, he realized that it would be necessary to overcome the mass error in the world by his final victory over death itself, through the demonstration of his own resurrection.

In these last days in Jerusalem, Jesus spent time giving his disciples much in the way of mystical teaching. Preparations were made by the little group to celebrate the Passover Feast in the guest chamber, a large upper room, in a private home. During this supper, Jesus indicated that this would be the last earthly meal he would have with them. He also told them that much of what he was going to teach they would not understand until after his death, when a great release of spiritual energy would activate the Holy Spirit. The Holy Spirit would illumine their hearts as to all the mystical teaching he would give this night. Up to this time the consciousness of what the Bible calls "gross darkness" had prevented the activity of the Holy Spirit on a universal scale. Although we are unable to explain this all scientifically, we do know that everything that exists does so in varying states of energy. In Truth, this is the Life of Spirit manifesting at varying vibratory rates. In matter, the vibratory rate has slowed down to such a pace that it is solidified. Jesus' spiritual work upon the world changed the vibratory rate. His was a single thrust in consciousness which released the power of the Holy Spirit, the Life and Activity of God. He talked much to his disciples about the Holy Spirit, the Comforter or Strengthener, who would come and lead them into all Truth.

His mystical teachings were accompanied by tangible acts to assist the learning process. One of these acts had to do with washing the disciples' feet, and he indicated that if their feet were clean they were clean all over. This teaching related Divine guidance in walking the earthly path. Paul was later to embellish this by saying that we should have our "feet shod with the preparation of the gospel of peace" (Eph. 6:15) so that we would have our walk in the awareness of being "fellow citizens with the saints, and of the household of God." (Eph. 2:19) This is the blessing of attunement with the Father, so that He can guide our paths into the way of peace and truth.

At this Passover Feast Jesus instituted a "New Passover." The old one had looked backward to the time that Moses, as God's instrument, had helped to liberate the Hebrew people from their Egyptian bondage. This "New Passover" looked forward to the liberation from a greater bondage, the freedom of the soul to live in the continued awareness of Spirit. In teaching them about the Oneness of Life, Jesus used bread and wine. In giving the bread he said, "Take, eat; this is my 'body.' " (This is the "Substance of God" which is given to your awareness through me.) He was telling them to assimilate Spirit Substance and to take it into their hearts, "feeding" upon it with thanksgiving. In giving them the wine he said, "This is my 'blood' (a symbol for life) of the New Testament, which is shed for many . . ." (Matt 26:26-28) He was telling them that he was the enabler of a New Age in consciousness that was going to assist them to know that the very Life of God (Cosmic Energy, Eternal Substance) was their life. By using elements that they could see, handle, touch and taste, he was conditioning their consciousness to union with God. He requested that this act be repeated in memory of him.

Another of the mystical teachings had to do with his not being with them anymore—as far as his physical presence was concerned. They were told that they would follow him later. "In my Father's house are many mansions (abiding places); if it were not so, I would have told you. I go to prepare a place for you. And if I go and prepare a place for you, I will come again, and receive you unto myself; that where I am, there ye may be also." (John 14:2-3) He was telling them that they would be where he was—in consciousness and would know all the joys of the Kingdom.

Philip, one of the disciples, said, "Shew us the Father, and it sufficeth us." He felt that if Jesus could somehow bring them straight into the face of the Father it would satisfy them, and they could accept all that he was telling them at this time. Jesus answered Philip by saying, "Have I been so long time with you, and yet hast thou not known me, Philip? He that hath seen me hath seen the Father, and how sayest thou then, Shew us the Father? Believest thou not that I am in the Father, and the Father in me? the words that I speak unto you I speak not of myself; but the Father that dwelleth in me, He doeth the works." (John 14:8-10) Again we see this mystical teaching of Oneness—the spirit of Truth made manifest in Jesus.

He opened before their spiritual vision a great panorama of accomplishment when he said that it was going to be *possible for them not only to do the works that he had done but to exceed them, because he was ascending to the Father.* "If ye love me, keep my commandments. And I will pray the Father, and He shall give you another Comforter, that He may abide with you forever; even the Spirit of Truth; whom the world cannot receive, because it seeth Him not, neither knoweth Him; but ye know Him; for He dwelleth with you, and shall be in you" (activated within you). (John 14:16-17) The immobilized consciousness of this time was unable to realize and perceive this personal activity of God. His disciples who had daily been with him during these three years had begun to grasp the concept of God WITH them; but the truth that God was WITHIN them, *expressing through them individually in the power of the Holy Spirit,* was to come into their experience at a later time, after Jesus' death.

Jesus realized that much of this mystical teaching would not be understood, so he continued, ". . . the Comforter, which is the Holy Ghost, whom the Father will send in my Name, He shall teach you all things, and bring all things to your remembrance, whatsoever I have said unto you. Peace I leave with you, my peace I give unto you . . . and now I have told you before it come to pass, that, when it is come to pass, ye might believe." Jesus desired that when this release of God's Energy came into the earth consciousness, they might attune themselves to it. He continued, "Hereafter I will not talk much with you: for the prince of this world cometh, and hath nothing in me." (John 14:26, 27, 29-30)

"The prince of this world" represented all forms of limitation, bondage and error. Jesus indicated that the mass error of the race consciousness could find nothing within his Being with which to attune itself. He was giving some teaching on the Law of Attraction. Our consciousness is like a magnet in many ways. It draws to us all the necessary situations that will assist our learning; and it repels all that is unlike itself. Jesus' consciousness was so attuned to the Father that no lesser, external appearance—no appearance of evil—had any claim upon him. It could find nothing in him by which to attach itself. Jesus was to give a further expansion on this magnetic Law of Attraction when he said "And I, if I be lifted up from the earth, will draw all men unto me." (John 12:32)

On this eventful night he gave them a new commandment that they "love one another, as I have loved you," explaining to them that "Greater love hath no man than this, that a man lay down his life for his friends." (John 15:12-13)

He also taught them the spiritual principle of abiding in the Perfection of that which Eternally IS—abiding in the life and consciousness of the Father. In his teaching on the vine and the branches he said "Abide in me, and I in you" (rest and live in my consciousness), . . . for without me (as I AM the expression of God) ye can do nothing." (John 15:4-5)

He said that he had spoken about all these things so that in the world of materiality and "mammon" they might have peace. "Be of good cheer; I have overcome the world." (John 16:33)

Read: John: Chapters 12, 13, 14, 15 and 16

CHAPTER X

The Drama of the Last Days
Part I

During the last days of his life, Jesus had wept over the City of Jerusalem. This religious capitol represented mankind's efforts to build a spiritual center—the Holy City—a place where it might find God. The efforts towards this establishment were all fixed in working through the externals of life. So much time had been given towards this project that the inner temple of Spirit had been sadly neglected, even overlooked. Jerusalem was actually a geographical place whose inhabitants were living in a consciousness of separation from their Creator. Jesus' whole thrust was toward oneness with God and the development of the "inner man."

Jesus wept over the city because he knew it would be destroyed. In his role as a prophet he could see its eventual downfall. It occurred 70 years later. He longed to see those about him illumined—ready to apply his teachings—for he knew that without their adherence to spiritual principle, the Law of Expression would prove itself faithful in bringing into manifestation that which was being sown through spiritual ignorance and darkness. He was facing earth's darkness and immobilized consciousness alone. There was no one to share this spiritual work. Since he was completely immersed in the Father, however, he was able to make this single thrust upon earth's consciousness which would energize the spiritual vibrations and direct them in a positive vein, so that the dormancy of God-activity could be released at Pentecost.

Long before his time the great prophets and seers had been able to dream dreams and foresee the final effect of God's perfection in manifestation among mankind. The Prophet Habakkuk said, "For the earth shall be filled with the KNOWLEDGE of the glory of the Lord as the waters cover the sea." (Hab. 2:14). Heaven was to be pressed out, or unfolded, into earth. Between the spiritual vision of the prophets and its actualization, however, a great gulf seemed to be fixed. While they could point to the end result and note the immobilized consciousness, they were unable individually to make the necessary impact upon it, to assist this activity into being. However, they had seen in the Messianic Hope, the Divine Agent of God, the fulfillment of their vision. Spirit would finally reign in the affairs of men and nations. Since the days of Adam and Eve, duality had reigned—one power pitted against another; but now as Jesus made final preparations for his death, the stage was set for the power of the Kingdom of God to manifest on earth.

Death would not have been inevitable for Jesus had he received the response to Truth that was necessary in order to *apply* the teaching. Humankind was yet unaware of its divine heredity, or God-Substance and God-Inherencies within.

Jesus still had the free-will opportunity to avoid his final sacrifice; and surely, he must have been tempted. His Gethsemane prayer carries overtones of a desire to escape this fate. "Father, if thou be willing, remove this cup from me: nevertheless not my will, but thine be done." (Luke 22:42) With the desire to be relieved of this Divine assignment, there was also the *balance* of complete relinquishment. It was a prayer that was in perfect alignment with the Father. This prayer was answered, not by removing the "cup," but by sending an "angel from heaven" to strengthen him. (Luke 22:43) We gain some insights into the Eternal importance of the Cross, as far as God's purposes for earth were concerned. Surely an all-loving Father-Mother God would never have permitted such a heinous crime to have been perpetrated unless it was necessary to bring ALL-Good to humanity. While we may not be able to fathom this Mystery, we do know Jesus' death on the Cross marked the beginning of his final victory of Spirit over matter.

The events in the life of one of Jesus' twelve disciples were also dramatically coming to a climax at this time. Judas Iscariot had become quite disenchanted with Jesus' humility and self-effacing attitude. Judas could not understand Jesus' refusal to use spiritual power to attain wealth, earthly power and self-aggrandizement. The Apostle John indicates that Judas exhibited the spirit of avarice as the keeper of the disciples' purse. While he pretended to include in this stewardship help for the poor, he actually had his own self interests at heart. (John 12:1-8)

Undoubtedly Judas had hoped that Jesus would use his power to overtake the Roman bondage. Had that occurred, Judas probably reasoned it would be politically expedient for him to get in on "the ground floor" with this new movement. As Jesus kept speaking to his disciples of his own impending death, this must have helped convince Judas that political and economic opportunities would not materialize. Thus he threw in his lot with the chief priests and scribes, offering them information as to Jesus' whereabouts, so that at the most expedient time the Master would be turned over to the authorities. Judas may have thought that this would help make him a national hero; and he may have been greedy for the thirty pieces of silver that were given to him in exchange for his help. The chief priests and scribes realized that taking Jesus on a feast day would cause an uproar among the people and bring the Roman authorities down upon them. So they worked with Judas in order to find the most expedient moment for the "arrest."

Jesus and his disciples celebrated the Feast of the Passover 24 hours before the actual time because the Master knew that things were moving rapidly now; and he had much to tell them in preparation for the dramatic climax which was at hand. Coupled with his mystical teachings of "oneness," Jesus also indicated that he was a realist as well as an Idealist. He knew that as soon as his disciples were removed from his consciousness, they would be unable to make the demonstrations that they had made while in his presence and under his personal influence. Up to now they had been doing their spiritual work in the light of his Light—and he needed to release them to work at their own level of awareness for awhile, *until his final work in consciousness* would provide the *enablement* for mankind *to work through the Holy Spirit within.* Jesus illustrated that we work at our own spiritual level of understanding, until illumined to allow Spirit to do the work through us. He said,

"When I sent you without purse, and scrip, and shoes, lacked ye any thing? And they said, Nothing. Then said he unto them, But now, he that hath a purse, let him take it, and likewise his scrip: and he that hath no sword, let him sell his garment, and buy one. For I say unto you, that this that is written must yet be accomplished in me, 'And he was reckoned among the transgressors': for the things concerning me have an end." (Luke 22:35-37)

As Wayshower, Jesus is telling us not to attempt demonstration beyond our spiritual understanding. We must have the commensurate consciousness to undergird what we bring to the word level of expression. While we carry on our spiritual work at our own pacing, it is not inevitable that we *stay* at a certain level of consciousness. *Daily exposure to the Father will assure inner changes and growth.*

After Jesus had completed what was necessary for his disciples at the Feast of the Passover, they sang a hymn and went to the Garden of Gethsemane, which lay at the foot of the Mount of Olives. This Garden is associated with the beginning of the physical, mental and spiritual suffering of Jesus. It was here in prayer that he began the great work in consciousness for the world, penetrating into all the mass error of the race consciousness and neutralizing it through the Truth of Spirit. While in communion with God for spiritual sustenance to carry through his spiritual work, he prayed a great prayer of oneness for the whole world. A study of John 17 indicates that the consciousness of duality was to come to an end. This prayer of Jesus, which is sometimes known as the "Great High Priestly Prayer" falls into three parts: (1) he prayed for himself, (2) he prayed for his disciples (in that Time dispensation), and (3) he prayed for his future disciples, which includes us who would be his disciples now. A study of this prayer shows it spiraling upwards in the Truth of Oneness and culminating in a final circle for all mankind—"That they ALL may be ONE."

When this part of Jesus' work was completed in prayer, Judas arrived on the scene with many people who were carrying swords and staves. With a kiss of betrayal Judas greeted Jesus with "Hail Master." Jesus had known for some time that Judas would betray him, but his reply to Judas was "FRIEND, wherefore art thou come?" (Matt. 26:50) He was offering his love and friendship to Judas and asking, "Why are you succumbing to the ways of the world? Why are you working against God? Why are you not flowing with the Eternal Tide of Spirit? Why are you selling out to spiritual captivity and bondage?"

The drama continues at this point as "Jesus . . . knowing all things that should come upon him, went forth, and said unto them, Whom seek ye? They answered him, Jesus of Nazareth. Jesus saith unto them, I am he. And Judas also, which betrayed him stood with them. As soon then as he had said unto them, I am he, they went backward, and fell to the ground. Then asked he them again, Whom seek ye? And they said, Jesus of Nazareth. Jesus answered, I have told you that I am he: if therefore ye seek me, let these go their way. That the saying might be fulfilled which he spake, Of them which thou gavest me have I lost none. Then Simon Peter having a sword drew it, and smote the high priest's servant, and cut off his right ear. The servant's name was Malchus. Then said Jesus unto Peter, Put up thy sword into the sheath: the cup which my Father hath given me, shall I not drink it?" (John 18:4-11)

The other Gospel accounts indicate that Jesus not only healed the man's ear, but that he underscored the Law of Expression to Peter: "All they that take the sword shall perish with the sword." (Matt. 26:52) The Master indicated that it was of his own free will that he was choosing the path of suffering and death. "Thinkest thou that I cannot *now* pray to my Father, and he shall *presently* give me more than twelve legions of angels?" (Matt 26:53) (Twelve is the number indicating completeness, and God would have granted Jesus complete and perfect protection from this trial had he requested it.) In explaining the *necessity* for giving of himself in death he went on to say that if he chose not to walk this path, "How then shall the scriptures be fulfilled, that thus it must be?" (Matt 26:54) Jesus desired that his followers realize that this was his divine destiny and that it had Eternal meaning and purpose in the Mind of God. He needed the agency of "death" not only to demonstrate the Resurrection, but also to *complete a great work in consciousness* that would *release and activate the Holy Spirit into the earth.*

Divine Science teaches that the knowledge which "enables mind to carry out its idea is perfect consciousness of God, the Holy Ghost." The Apostle John tells us that this aspect of God (the Holy Ghost) "was *not yet given*; because that Jesus was *not yet glorified.*" (John 7:39) We can later trace the impact of the activation of the Holy Spirit of God as it occurred within 120 disciples after Jesus' death. They were instantaneously illumined and empowered.

As the appearances of evil seemed to be more and more in control, all of the twelve disciples, with the exception of John, were to leave Jesus, as the Master had foretold. Also true to his prophecies, Peter would deny him three times. John alone remained and was an eyewitness to the rest of the drama.

Jesus was taken, bound, from the Garden of Gethsemane by a guard of soldiers to Annas, the father-in-law of Caiaphas, the high priest. In this high priestly family Annas must still have been considered as the voice of authority, even though Caiaphas was actually the one holding the office of High Priest that year. In the presence of Annas, every attempt was made to manufacture a case against Jesus that would warrant the death penalty. As we watch Jesus during this trial, he shows us the way to handle such crises in life by utilizing three spiritual principles: (1) *Jesus made a point of not defending himself.* Defending the personality can make one vulnerable to further accusation, and the vision becomes focused on the lesser self. (2) *He remained silent at the appropriate times.* There is a time to speak and a time to be silent. Attunement with the Father will cause us to make the best use of our words. (3) *He did not entangle himself with argument.* By not identifying with the false accusations of his enemies he did not waste or dissipate his Divine Substance. He maintained a fixed and steadfast consciousness, poised in the Truth that "the Father and I are one" at all times.

Only the human, imperfect personality wishes to retaliate. Jesus' personality was perfectly integrated with his Individuality. He had made it clear to his enemies that "this is your hour, and the power of darkness." (Luke 22:53)

When Annas continued to question Jesus about his teaching, the Master realized that it would do no good to give a lengthy discourse on the Kingdom. He did say that he had daily taught openly in the Temple, or the synagogue where all the Jews met, and that none of his activities was performed secretly. He suggested that Annas question those who had heard him teach. (John 18:20-21) One of the officers became very antagonized at this answer and slapped Jesus. This assault and the whole ecclesiastical trial in the middle of the night were highly irregular and probably illegal. Jesus' response to this indignity was nonretaliatory. He did not use the working method of his opponents. Paul was later to receive the same kind of treatment when he was establishing the truth of the Christian faith; but he did not respond at the same spiritual level as Jesus. Paul's response definitely carried overtones of retaliation. "God shall smite thee, thou whited wall: for sittest thou to judge me after the law, and commandest me to be smitten contrary to the law?" (Acts 23:3) Jesus, however, was demonstrating his own mystical teaching in such circumstances— "Agree with thine adversary quickly" (Matt. 5:25)—which prevents our consciousness from becoming entangled with our opponents'.

In building a case against Jesus, false witnesses were brought in; their stories did not agree. Certain of these witnesses said, "We heard him say, I will destroy this temple that is made with hands, and within three days I will build another made without hands." (Mark 14:58) The high priest requested Jesus to answer to these charges, but JESUS REMAINED SILENT AND HELD HIS PEACE. He did not try to explain how they had misinterpreted his original teaching— that although his body (the physical "Temple of God") should be destroyed, he would raise it up in three days (the Resurrection). They were not only in a spiritual state unready to understand, but they were *unwilling* even to ponder it. Finally the high priest said, "Art thou the Christ, the Son of the Blessed? And Jesus said, I am; and ye shall see the Son of man sitting on the right hand of power, and coming in the clouds of heaven"—overcoming the world of appearances. (Mark 14:61-62)

Jesus' answer brought the trial to a close. The needed evidence had been given. His answer constituted blasphemy, a crime guilty of the death penalty. The high priest rent his clothes—an outer ritual which would appear to be righteous indignation, but in his heart he did not know the living God.

While this ecclesiastical trial had found Jesus guilty, his accusers did not have the power to carry out the death penalty. Therefore he was taken to the Roman governor, Pontius Pilate, so that orders for this execution might come from Rome. Pilate could find no charges that were worthy of the death sentence, and at one point told the Jews to settle the matter among themselves. The Jews were insistent that the interrogations continue. During this time Pilate discovered that Jesus was a Galilean, and therefore subject to Herod Antipas' jurisdiction. Jesus was sent to Herod who was very glad to see him, for he thought perhaps the Master would perform some miracle. To Herod's questions JESUS ANSWERED NOTHING. Jesus was finally humiliated by Herod and his men, who put a gorgeous robe on him and sent him back to Pilate.

As Jesus continued with Pilate, we find him answering some of Pilate's questions. He undoubtedly recognized a little more depth in Pilate than in Herod. The accusations against Jesus by the rulers and the chief priests centered around his perverting the nation, refusing to give tribute to Caesar, and claiming to be a king. When Pilate asked about the claims to being a king, Jesus went on to tell him, "My Kingdom is not of this world: if my Kingdom were of this world, then would my servants fight, that I should not be delivered to the Jews: but now is my Kingdom not from hence. Pilate therefore said unto him, Art thou a king then? Jesus answered, Thou sayest, that I am, a king. To this end was I born, and for this cause came I into the world that I should bear witness unto the Truth. Everyone that is of the Truth heareth my voice. Pilate saith unto him, What is Truth? And when he had said this, he went out again unto the Jews, and saith unto them, I find in him no fault at all." (John 18:38)

One wonders what unfoldment might have occurred in Pilate had he stayed and allowed Jesus to answer the question, "What is Truth?" The Truth Jesus spoke had to do with Reality breaking through to the true knowledge of God and man—the Basis of our being. "In Him, (God) we live and move and have our being." (Acts 17:28) It had to do with looking through the distorted world of appearances dominated by fear, greed and error, and seeing the Eternal—the Father, who "giveth to ALL life and breath and ALL THINGS." (Acts 17:25) The Kingdom of Love, Life and Light was awaiting those of Jesus' day—just as it awaits those of our day. What he could not do in life to assist mankind to enter it, he would do through death, resurrection and ascension.

READ: John, Chapters 17 and 18. Mark, Chapter 14.

> *Divine Science: Its Principle and Practice*, Page 61. Divine Science Publication.
>
> Alkins: *Bridge Builders of Truth* (The Question of Jesus). Divine Science Publication.

CHAPTER XI

The Drama of the Last Days
Part II

When Pilate reported to the Jews that he could find no fault in Jesus worthy of the death penalty, he reminded them of a custom: one Jewish prisoner was released each year at Passover time. Pilate asked, "Will ye therefore that I release unto you the King of the Jews? Then cried they all again, saying, Not this man, but Barabbas." (John 18:38-40) Barabbus had been in prison, charged with robbery, insurrection and murder. He represents the symbol of hatred, violence, greed and rebellion in the world of duality. In our own time he has been released in race riots, crime, violence and murder—sometimes under the guise of improving the human lot. Barabbus' way of dealing with the world's problems was in direct contrast to Jesus' method. Barabbus worked from the externals of life, forcing the issues, crushing individuals in order to gain his own ends. In dealing with the vital issues of the world today, that same question is being asked of us—"Shall I release unto you, Jesus the Christ, or Barabbus?" Each has his followers. Many work exclusively with the externals of life for profit and gain, while some seek to follow the ways of Truth as set forth by Jesus the Wayshower.

The crowds at that time chose that Barabbus should be set free, and that the Christ should die. Pilate ordered that Jesus be scourged—flogged and whipped with a lash impregnated with sharp pieces of metal. The soldiers made a crown of twigs and thorns that pierced his flesh as it was placed on his head in mockery. He was clothed in a purple robe, slapped in the face, and openly humiliated. Had he been centered in his own personality, Jesus could have broken. Pilate again went out to the people, taking the Christ who was clothed in the purple robe and wearing the crown of thorns. Again the Roman governor said that he could find nothing worthy of death in Jesus. The crowds, worked up into a frenzy at the sight of Jesus, cried out "Crucify him, crucify him." Pilate's hesitancy caused the Jews to tell him that they had a law which *required* Jesus' death, because the Master had made himself out to be the Son of God. Jesus was charged with blasphemy. (John 19:2-7)

Hearing this reply Pilate became uneasy and fearful. The wrath of the crowd made him realize that he could not ignore their commands. At the same time Pilate must have been thinking of the warning that had been given to his wife in a dream, that he "have . . . nothing to do with that just man, for I have suffered many things this day in a dream because of him." (Matt. 27:19) In his uneasiness, Pilate asked Jesus where he was *really* from. When Jesus gave him no reply, Pilate said "Speakest thou not unto me? knowest thou not that I have power to crucify thee, and have power to release thee?" Pilate wanted Jesus to realize the authority that was vested in a Roman governor. To this Jesus replied "Thou couldest have no power at all against me, except it were given thee from above; therefore he (who of his own free will) that delivered me unto thee hath the greater sin." (John 19:8-11)

We shall never have to face the seemingly insurmountable odds that Jesus did, but it is well for us to realize these words of power and truth in the face of difficulties. "This difficulty or obstacle on the path has NO POWER at all against me except what is given from above—except for how this situation will be used to serve God's purposes." Jesus—in his teaching and by his own demonstration—shows us the necessity to come into total alignment with the truth that the Lord God, Omnipotent, reigns!

Pilate sought to release Jesus but the Jews threatened him by saying, "If thou let this man go, thou art not Caesar's friend: whosoever maketh himself a king speaketh against Caesar." Pilate became a pawn of duality—one power pitted against another. When he had led Jesus out to the judgment seat he said "Behold your King!" At these words "they cried out, Away with him, away with him, crucify him. Pilate saith unto them, Shall I crucify your King? The chief priests answered, We have no king but Caesar." (John 19:12-15) Pilate then handed Jesus over to them to be crucified.

"We have no king but Caesar." This is the tribute of unillumined consciousness to *materiality*. For one to be King of the Light would mean that he would neutralize the darkened states of consciousness and therefore be anti-Caesar. He would not be giving power to the *effects* of life. Rather, he would be *releasing* those who all their lives had been in bondage to false beliefs and false gods. Those who choose "Caesar" as king serve only the things which they can see and hear and touch in the outer appearances of life. In futility they serve; in spiritual ignorance they refuse to become subject to the Divine Idea.

As Jesus was first brought to civil trial, Judas Iscariot, the Master's betrayor, came into the realization that he had betrayed innocent life. It may be that he had not thought things would be carried this far—that perhaps if he forced Jesus' hand the Master would exercise supreme power in overcoming his enemies, and at the same time lead an insurrection against Rome. In remorse Judas returned the thirty pieces of silver to the chief priests and elders, telling them that he had done wrong. "And they said What is that to us? See thou to that." "And he (Judas) cast down the pieces of silver in the temple, and departed, and went and hanged himself." (Matt. 27:4-5)

To Judas, "Caesar" had been king. He had paid his tributes to materiality—to the *effects* of life. At the time of supreme crisis in Judas' life, "Caesar" had failed to comfort and uphold him. Jesus alone had truly cared for him. Had Judas allowed the Christ to illumine him, he could have been spared the consequences of his tragic mistake. We cannot place our reliance in person, place or thing. There is only One worthy of our complete trust and faith. Jesus teaches us to "Have faith in *God*"—the FIRST CAUSE of all Life.

The means of execution for the Jews was stoning. For the Romans it was crucifixion. The scourging (being beaten with loaded whips) preceded the execution. Crucifixion was described by Cicero as "the most cruel and hideous of punishments."

After the scourging, the physical and emotional abuse, and being denied any sleep throughout the whole night, Jesus was required to carry the crossbeam of his own cross to the place of execution—Golgotha, or as Luke names it, Calvary. When he fell to the ground at one point along the way, a Cyrenian named Simon was commanded to carry the cross.

Along the way there were some observers who expressed compassion and concern for the Master. Some of the women were crying. "But Jesus turning unto them said, Daughters of Jerusalem, weep not for me, but weep for yourselves, and for your children." He said that the days were coming when it would be considered fortunate to be childless. "Then shall they begin to say to the mountains, Fall on us; and to the hills, Cover us. For if they do these things in a green tree, what shall be done in the dry?" (Luke 23:27-31) In his role as prophet and teacher, Jesus clearly saw the events that would lead to the destruction of Jerusalem in 70 A.D. He was urging these women to apply his teachings; to turn their attention and allegiance to God, and thus avert this tragedy. His concern was never for himself, but always for others. Through every moment of his life—even while walking this road to Calvary—he was ministering the Word of God, the creative energy of Spirit.

Jesus was crucified between two thieves. Pilate ordered that a title be written out and "put on the cross. And the writing was JESUS OF NAZARETH, THE KING OF THE JEWS. This title then read many of the Jews: for the place where Jesus was crucified was nigh to the city: and it was written in Hebrew, and Greek, and Latin. Then said the chief priests of the Jews to Pilate, Write not, The King of the Jews; but that he said, I am King of the Jews. Pilate answered, What I have written I have written. Then the soldiers, when they had crucified Jesus, took his garments, and made four parts, to every soldier a part; and also his coat. Now the coat was without seam, woven from the top throughout. They said therefore among themselves, Let us not rend it, but cast lots for it, whose it shall be." (John 19:18-24) This detail concerning the death of the Messiah had been written in the sacred scriptures by the Psalmist hundreds of years before. "They pierced my hands and my feet. They part my garments among them, and cast lots upon my vesture." (Ps. 22:16, 18)

As John continues with his account of the Crucifixion he tells us that "there stood by the cross of Jesus his mother, and his mother's sister, Mary the wife of Cleophas, and Mary Magdalene. When Jesus therefore saw his mother, and the disciple (John) standing by, whom he loved, he saith unto his mother, Woman, behold thy son! Then saith he to the disciple. Behold thy mother! And from that hour that disciple took her unto his own home." (John 19:25-27) John alone stayed by the Cross. All the other disciples had fled, just as Jesus had foreseen.

Often through our own hours of soul "travail" we can find ourselves alone except for a "John" and a "Mary." Jesus the Wayshower always urges us to love the people in our lives, but never to be dependent upon them. The Master drew his sustenance for all of life's events from the Father. He made his identity with people through the Father within them, but knew that their yet-undeveloped personalities would not be capable of spiritually understanding or walking his path with him.

During a crucifixion the victim was sometimes offered drugged wine. In Jesus' case it was vinegar mixed with gall, but he refused it. Psalm 69:21 prophesied this detail long before— "They gave me also gall for my meat and in my thirst they gave me vinegar to drink." The Psalmist had also recorded the taunts and jeers of the chief priests, scribes, elders and other onlookers: "And they that see me laugh me to scorn: they shoot out the lip, they shake the head, saying he trusted on the Lord that he would deliver him; let him deliver him, seeing he delighted in him." (Ps. 22:7-8)

The onlookers in fulfillment of prophecy said: "Thou that destroyest the temple, and buildest it in three days, save thyself. If thou be the Son of God, come down from the cross. Likewise also the chief priests mocking him, with the scribes and elders said, He saved others; himself he cannot save. If he be the King of Israel, let him now come down from the cross, and we will believe him. He trusted in God; let him deliver him now, if he will have him: for he said I am the Son of God. The thieves

also, which were crucified with him, cast the same in his teeth."
(Matt. 27:39-44)

One of the thieves who was crucified with him appealed to
him to save himself and to also save them if he was the Christ.
The other thief said, "We receive the due reward of our deeds;
but this man hath done nothing amiss. And he said unto Jesus,
Lord, remember me when thou comest into thy Kingdom. And
Jesus said unto him, Verily I say unto thee, TODAY shalt thou
be with me in Paradise." (Luke 23:39-43) In using the words
TODAY and PARADISE Jesus shattered two dreaded false
beliefs about death. He had told this man that there is life
beyond this mortal one—that it is continuous and ongoing
(Today)—and that they would not be entering a dreaded
darkness, but rather a higher plane of consciousness offering
growth and more light (Paradise).

The Crucifixion of Jesus began at nine in the morning. He
lived on the cross for six hours. Mark records three hours of
darkness over the land. Toward the end of his ordeal Jesus
cried out, "My God, my God, why hast thou forsaken me?"
The Aramaic interpretation, according to Laamsa's translation,
is: "My God, my God, *for this was I spared.*"* Reading this
meaning into these words, Jesus is again saying that his life is
his gift to humanity. He is giving himself as an agent of
deliverance from limitation and bondage. As the end of his
suffering grew near he cried out with a loud voice, "Father, into
thy hands I commend my spirit," accompanying them with, "It
is finished." At that point a Roman centurion who was standing
by said, "Truly this man was the Son of God."

The evening of the crucifixion was Friday—not only the
preparation for the Jews' Sabbath, but also the preparation for
their Paschal Feast. Being superstitious and subject to primitive
beliefs that a curse would be brought upon the land if the
corpses hung on the crosses over night, the Jews urged Pilate to
remove them. Even death had to fit into their time frames, for
they asked that Pilate hasten death (if it had not already
occurred) by breaking the legs of the victims. The soldiers
broke the legs of the two thieves, but when they came to Jesus

they were sure that he was already dead. (An ancient prophecy had said that "none of his (Messiah's) bones shall be broken.") One of the soldiers took his sword and pierced Jesus' side.

Joseph of Arimathea, a very rich man and a member of the Sanhedrin, had been a follower of Jesus. With great courage he came to Pilate and asked for Jesus' body. Since the chief priests and elders were determined to wipe out the whole Jesus movement, Joseph was placing his own life in danger. Joseph did exercise the precaution of coming to Pilate secretly. Another follower of Jesus, a Pharisee named Nicodemus, brought spices; and the body was anointed, wrapped in linen, and placed in a new sepulchre that belonged to Joseph.

It is impossible to try to fathom the mystery of the Crucifixion. To gain further insights as to God's purposes in it, there is yet much more to be revealed to our understanding. This much we do know. Jesus did not die. He only TASTED death. Furthermore, he declared "And I, if I be lifted up from the earth, will draw all men (humanity) unto me." (John 12:32) As the Christ, he was to be a magnetic, cosmic influence!

READ: Matt. 27:1-66; Mark 15:1-47; John 19:1-42

*George M. Laamsa, *Holy Bible from Ancient Eastern Manuscripts*. Publisher: A.J. Holman Company, Philadelphia.

CHAPTER XII

Post-Resurrection Appearances

One may gain some deeper insights into the life, death and resurrection of Jesus by studying the works of Emma Curtis Hopkins, the "teacher of the teachers" in the New Thought Movement. In her work *High Mysticism**, she makes reference to many illumined souls before Jesus' time—Gautama Buddha, Elijah, Elisha, to name a few—who desired vicariously to do the soul work of others around them by releasing them from the bondage of sickness and death. Since they were not sufficiently identified with "Divinity Supreme," they were unable to do a mass-consciousness, corporate work that would so energize the dormant God-powers within humanity as to neutralize the effects of sin, error and limitation. Hopkins concludes that "it is only Jesus of Nazareth in the history of man, who has understood how to consciously withdraw the wretchedness of the people into Himself, and make wretchednes nothing, both for them and for Himself."

The drama of Jesus' work unfolds after his body had been properly prepared and placed in a sepulchre hewn from rock. The chief priests, recalling that there were many rumors that he would rise from the dead, decided that perhaps his own disciples might come and steal the body away and then tell the people that Jesus had performed the supreme miracle—that of energizing his own body and overcoming death. They therefore requested that Pilate place a large stone at the entry of the sepulchre and seal it. To doubly insure that no one would have access to the body, they also requested that a guard of soldiers be kept at the site to watch until the third day. Jesus had said that he would rise on the third day, and although they did not believe him, they did not want anyone to tamper with the body in order to substantiate the Master's claims.

On the first day of the week (Sunday), Mary Magdalene, Mary the mother of James, and some other women went to the sepulchre to anoint the body. They had some concerns about gaining entrance. They knew that the stone would have to be removed, and questioned whether the guard of soldiers would cooperate with their desires. Matthew goes on to record supernatural happenings which occurred then. He says that there was an "earthquake" (undoubtedly some physical sound and a movement of the earth)—and "an angel" (a supernatural being) descended and rolled away the stone and sat upon it. This being was described as having a countenance like lightning and raiment which was as white as snow. So momentous was the event that the guards at the tomb were paralyzed with fear. The angel spoke to the women, calming them and telling them not to be afraid; for Jesus whom they were seeking had risen from the dead. His body was not in the tomb! They were directed to go and tell the startling news to his disciples that he had resurrected his body and was going before them into Galilee. They would see him there. As Mary Magdalene ran ahead and found Simon Peter and John, she must have been in a state of shock, for she could not comprehend all that the angel had disclosed to her and her companions. The Resurrection was beyond human belief—a first—completely out of the range of the "miracles" she had witnessed through Jesus' ministry. Though Jesus had raised Lazarus from the dead, it had never really occurred to them that Jesus could raise himself!

Peter and John came to the sepulchre and saw only the linen grave clothes lying where the body had been. After they left, Mary Magdalene stood outside the sepulchre weeping. When she looked into the sepulchre she saw two angels, one standing at the head and one at the feet where Jesus' body had lain. When they asked her why she was crying she said, "Because they have taken away my Lord, and I know not where they have laid him." (John 20:13) She could not grasp the truth of the Resurrection. Under the same circumstances we would likely have the same reaction. We would not be able to believe that a loved one who died could literally raise or energize the corpse! Only when Jesus personally appeared to her, her awareness expanded.

John and Peter had noticed that the linen grave clothes were lying in the sepulchre in the same position as when they had been on the corpse. The linen napkin (or headpiece), separate from the body pieces, lay on the resting place for the head. The men realized that the position of the linens indicated that the body had not been stolen away, but that it had been energized away from the shroud.

Peter and John excitedly left the site to share this news with the other followers of Jesus; and Mary Magdalene, who stayed on the scene, then met the Resurrected Christ. She did not recognize him at first and thought him to be the gardener, until he called her by name—"Mary." He may have been in an etheric bodily form which she did not comprehend at first glance. When she heard his voice she immediately responded with "Master." "Jesus saith unto her, Touch me not; for I am not yet ascended to my Father; but go to my brethren, and say unto them, I ascend unto my Father, and your Father; and to my God, and your God." (John 20:17) These words were not meant to be understood in a physical sense, for further records indicate that the disciples did touch him. He implied to Mary that the spiritual process was not completed; and he was also asking her not to circumscribe him in her former limited consciousness of him. In other words "Cease clinging to Me or holding Me in the consciousness of an earthly body. I function now in a different form. You must release all your cherished beliefs, and open your mind and heart to a greater revelation of Truth. After I have fully ascended to my Father you may be able to view Me with the outer physical eye, but you will know Me and My activity more fully through the *inner visional soul faculty*. You must turn *within* to view Me."

Jesus the Wayshower is always stimulating us to open our spiritual eyes and to unplug the spiritual auditory channels—to use and sensitize the inner spiritual avenues of communication, so that we may perceive the world of Spirit through the world of appearances.

The world of appearances had not only deceived Mary Magdalene, but Jesus' other followers as well, *and had he not broken through them,* they could never have accepted his

Resurrection. The same day that Jesus caused Reality to break through to Mary Magdalene, two of his other followers were walking to Emmaus, a village close to Jerusalem. Their conversation was filled with sadness and confusion. Jesus came and walked along beside them but they did not recognize him. He inquired as to their conversation, and they told him that he must be the only person in Jerusalem who had not heard of how the chief priests and rulers had handed their Master over for execution. They went on to say that if that hadn't been enough, they were now disturbed because some of their womenfolk were claiming to have had a vision of angels who said that Jesus was alive. They told Jesus that while some of their people had gone off to the tomb and found things just as the women had said, they did not see Jesus. (Luke 24:13-24) These followers, too, were bound in a prison of logic, reason, deduction and the world of appearances. They could not let their minds be influenced by what they must have thought to be unreasonable ideas.

Finally Jesus spoke to them and said "O . . . slow of heart to believe all that the prophets have spoken: Ought not Christ to have suffered these things, and to enter into his glory?And BEGINNING AT MOSES AND ALL THE PROPHETS, HE EXPOUNDED UNTO THEM IN ALL THE SCRIPTURES THE THINGS CONCERNING HIMSELF." They invited Jesus to go into a house with them, still not recognizing him. It was while he sat at a table, took a loaf of bread and gave thanks, that the illumination came to them as to who this "stranger" was. Their spiritual eyes opened—their understanding was illumined. As they discussed this together, they said that this revelation had been preceded by a glow in their hearts as he was walking with them on the road, and *opening to their understanding the meaning of the Scriptures,* which they had *read all their lives, yet failed to comprehend.*

These two followers returned to Jerusalem within the same hour and found Jesus' eleven disciples, telling them about the Master's appearance to them. As they were speaking, Jesus appeared again in their midst saying, "Peace be unto you." The world of appearances again closed in and they were terrified, fearing that they were seeing a spirit or a ghost. Then he asked them why they were so troubled and why such thoughts arose in their hearts. To prove that he was not an apparition, he invited them to look at his hands and his feet—to handle them and see; for "a spirit hath not flesh and bones, as ye see me have." (Luke 24:13-39)

As the Wayshower of what is beyond the grave, Jesus gives us some insights into our own transition. We shall be functioning on a different wave length than earth dwellers, but at the same time in that "mighty cloud of witnesses" which the Hebrew writer tells us surrounds those who are on the earth journey. (Heb. 12:1-2)

One of the disciples, Thomas, was not present when Jesus transmitted the peace of his consciousness upon his followers. When he heard what had happened he said that unless he could see this with his own eyes, and feel Jesus with his own hands, he would not accept what they had told him. A week later (on a Sunday) when they were again gathered together, Jesus appeared in their midst. Thomas was invited to touch and not doubt, but believe. The world of tangibility was accommodating the world of Spirit, and Thomas expressed complete belief. Jesus said that Thomas was blessed by that belief, and then went on to say, "Thomas, because thou hast seen me, thou hast believed: blessed are they that have not seen, and yet have believed." (John 20:24-29)

We are told by the Apostle John that Jesus demonstrated many other signs in the presence of his disciples which are not recorded in his gospel, but he felt that he had recorded enough for us who were not eyewitnesses of these events. The records of his gospel, he felt, would assist us to believe and to know this "blessedness" in believing. (John 20:30-31) John ends his gospel by saying, "And there are also many other things which Jesus did, the which, if they should be written every one, could not contain the books that should be written"—too numerous to attempt to record. (John 21:25)

During the forty days after the Resurrection, Jesus appeared to his followers many times. He had promised to go ahead of them into Galilee. This he did, and when they were at Tiberias, fishing and catching nothing, Jesus stood on the shore again unrecognized by them. He called out to them, asking if they had caught anything. When they let him know of their poor luck he instructed them to throw the net on the right side of the boat, and assured them that if they did this they would catch something. Following his instructions they had a net full of fish. When this "miracle" occurred it was John who said, "It is the Lord." "When Simon Peter heard that it was the Lord, he girt his fisher's coat unto him, (for he was naked), and did cast himself into the sea. And the other disciples came in a little ship; (for they were not far from land, but as it were two hundred cubits), dragging the net with fishes. As soon then as they were come to land, they saw a fire of coals there, and fish laid thereon, and bread. Jesus saith unto them, Bring of the fish which ye have now caught. Simon Peter went up, and drew the net to land, full of great fishes, an hundred and fifty and three: and for all there were so many, yet was not the net broken." (John 21:1-11) Jesus invited them to come and eat the bread and fish. They all recognized him through these common acts of everyday life.

Jesus as Wayshower is teaching us to view every moment of life as sacred—to regard every earthly act and happening as an opportunity to have Reality break through for us and to recognize Christ. He worked through the natural to the supernatural, reconciling them in Oneness. If we approach all of life in what the writer to the Hebrews calls "brotherly love," we may, through offering hospitality to strangers, be entertaining "angels unawares." (Heb. 13:1-2) The world of Reality is ever pressing through the natural world; and we never know, in a sudden moment while working at an earthly task, when we shall come into a deeper encounter with God. He shall be more real to us than the created world around us.

Before Jesus' crucifixion, Peter had denied him three times—as the Master had prophesied. One would think that Peter had regressed spiritually, for he had gone from that illumined time when he declared to Jesus, "Thou art the Christ, the son of the living God," to complete denial of Jesus when the going got rough. This has happened to many of us; often we become impatient with our delays in unfolding. The compassion of Jesus reached out immediately to Peter, however, as he ministered to him after they had eaten breakfast on the shores of the Lake of Galilee. (John 21:15-17) "So when they had dined, Jesus saith to Simon Peter, Simon, son of Jonas, lovest thou me more than these?" (more than the purposes of the world). "He (Peter) saith unto him, Yea, Lord; thou knowest that I love thee. He saith unto him, Feed my lambs" (the neophytes in the life of Spirit). "He saith to him again the second time, Simon, son of Jonas, lovest thou me?" (Do you love me unconditionally for myself alone?) "He (Peter) saith unto him, Yea, Lord; thou knowest that I love thee. He saith unto him, Feed my sheep." (the more mature souls in the life of Spirit). "He saith unto him the third time, Simon, son of Jonas, lovest thou me? Peter was grieved because he said unto him the third time, Lovest thou me? And he said unto him, Lord, thou knowest all things; thou knowest that I love thee." (You already can discern the innermost thoughts that I have— you know my inner man). "Jesus saith unto him, Feed my sheep," (all those who are seeking the Kingdom of God and its Righteousness). Peter had formerly denied Jesus three times. Now he was given a three-fold reinstatement through those three questions and directions.

Jesus recognized Peter's special work for the Kingdom and so relieved him of any sense of guilt or condemnation for having failed. He reinstated him to his rightful place in his soul journey and blessed him on his way. Had Peter not received this spiritual treatment from Jesus, guilt and self-condemnation would have deterred his soul journey, and his divinely appointed work. Failures and weaknesses of the personality are always covered by the strength and guidance of the Holy Spirit within. Jesus' mission as Wayshower is ever to lift us to our rightful place, to remind us of our divine heredity, and to assure us that we have inner programming for Perfection. (Matt. 5:48)

The influence of Jesus the Wayshower has revealed the truth of the relationship between Man and God; has declared Man's

CHAPTER XIII

Personal Identification and Relationship with God:
Our Father Which Art in Heaven

As we expand our awareness of LIFE in any form, we find ourselves dealing with three factors: (1) The ultimate *body of known knowledge* concerning what IS; (2) our *level of understanding* of that knowledge, and (3) *the ability to apply* it to our daily living. In all stages of learning we are attempting to bridge what might appear to be a gap, by expanding our understanding to the point whereby we may completely internalize and utilize our knowledge. Until we can appropriate it fully, we experience limitations in the application—and the by-products of it.

Jesus the Wayshower is the BRIDGE between what Eternally IS—and the point of our individual awareness. He served as that BRIDGE by submitting himself to the limitations of matter, and by demonstrating a complete overcoming through his Life, Death and Resurrection. He also serves as a BRIDGE through his influence and his teaching—which at the beginning of our quest are seedbeds of Truth, becoming ever-expanding avenues of awareness to the Perfection of God who Eternally IS.

Until our awareness of the totality of life is expanded, we are confined to the limitations of appearances. At one time we believed that the world was flat because appearance seemed so to indicate. Accepting this appearance as truth, mankind was confined to small geographical areas and stayed physically in one place. We denied ourselves opportunities to explore, to share and to experience the larger world beyond.

In our goal of working cooperatively together with God, He is leading us into all Truth. Jesus the Wayshower reveals to us, in the totality of his teaching, that every problem we face, every lack or limitation, is there because we do not allow Reality to press through. Our real need is to become aware of the Omnipresence of God working through every detail of our lives. There are cardinal principles, which Jesus reiterates, concerning the relationship of Man and God: Man's dominion, Kingdom manifestations, liberation, supply, release, Divine protection, and the establishment of the Christ Consciousness. These principles will be developed in the remaining chapters through the teachings in the Lord's Prayer (Matt. 6:9-13)—part of the Divine Roadmap given by the Master in the Sermon on the Mount. (Matt. 5, 6, 7)

For Jesus it was not difficult to accept the Reality of Omnipresence and the truth of God's Word as spoken through the Prophet Jeremiah: "Am I a God at hand . . . and not a God far off? Can any hide himself in secret places that I shall not see him? Do not I FILL Heaven and earth?" The word "fill" infers that the Substance of God is enfolded in all space, infilling the most minute particle of what we refer to as matter. Since He FILLS Heaven and earth, there is no place where God is not. He is equally, everywhere present, in all, through all, filling all. (Jer. 23:24; Eph. 4:6)

As he looked down the corridors of Time, Jesus realized that there would come a day when earth's inhabitants would be immersed in the Truth of God Omnipresent, Omnipotent and Omniscient. He foresaw, as did the prophets before him, a time when spiritual awareness would expand to realize, and to be immersed in, the KNOWLEDGE of God. (John 17:3)

As the Wayshower, Jesus bridged a centuries-long gap between the vision of the prophets, and actualization. As a Master Teacher he not only gives us a perfect scope and sequence of spiritual instruction; but in essence, the perfect prayer. In the Lord's Prayer he places each statement of Truth in its proper order of importance, climaxing it by a Jewish doxology of praise: "For THINE is the Kingdom, the Power and the Glory FOREVER." As the basis of ALL—and as the central chord uniting ALL—he begins the prayer with the underlying theme which gives meaning and relevance to the whole teaching—OUR FATHER. These two words communicate the intimacy of *a personal identification of all mankind with God.*

Some of us have been raised with a concept of God quite opposite from the Master's own teaching. We hope to outgrow it as we evolve in Truth; yet we shall continue to encounter in the race consciousness the belief in a God of separation, not Oneness; in a Creator detached from His Creation, not infused in it; of a God "outside" us, rather than a God who is both transcendent and immanent—"who is *above all*, and *through all*, and *in you all*" (Eph. 4:6)—a God *within* who is *equally everywhere present*. We ourselves may have to condition our subconscious continually with this vital truth of Omnipresence; for the subconscious must be cleansed and redeemed from the mass error of the world. Jesus the Wayshower says that the eye of the soul must be single, so that our body may be filled with Light. (Matt. 6:22) We must wash away every trace of the consciousness of separation as we meditate on the universality of the words "OUR Father."

When we know "Our Father" as Perfect Love, Light and Truth and realize that we are poised in His Life, we are cradled in Omnipresence. "Our Father" offers us spiritual freedom. As His creation, *we are made in His image and likeness;* and therefore *possess a divine heredity* which is to be *activated by His Holy Spirit within us.* As this divine heredity (the Christ within us) is allowed to express, the lesser self (the personality) becomes subject to the Christ. God, our Father, is the only Reality. He expresses *through us* and *as us.* We are *individualized* expressions of God, each an important Life-Cell of the Infinite One, the Source of all that is.

Jesus knew that *personal identification with God* would bring the majesty and power of Divinity into focus. We may be well versed in stating the spiritual laws of the universe, we may be able to affirm intellectually many great statements of Truth; but if these segments of knowledge are not intrinsically bound to a PERSONAL RELATIONSHIP with "Our Father," they tend to remain as little more than intellectual exercises—lacking spiritual power. Jesus was vitally interested in presenting Truth which could be *applied*, and he realized that at the very heart of the matter lay this personal relationship with God. The application phase of the teaching comes in the *practice of the Presence of God*, as "Our Father."

Through experiencing God as "Our Father," we automatically expand and enrich our communion with all of His Creation. The Apostle John embellished this teaching. He says that it is impossible to love God and yet hate one's brother.

Sometimes people who are knowledgeable in the teachings of Jesus, and promoters of Christianity, abdicate in times of trouble. They lack this personal relationship—and find it impossible to practice or realize the Presence of God as Reality. As they walk the "deep waters," they turn away from God (in awareness) and are unable to gain spiritual insights in their "walk." Unfortunately they really do not *know* God—they only know *about* Him through a body of knowledge. Others, who balance their spiritual study with a personal relationship, see obstacles on the path as temporary, as challenges to apply Truth and overcome. They have an unshakable faith that God will undertake for them and perfect all that concerns them. We could liken *spiritual knowledge* to a human "skeleton"—necessary for the bodily framework; but a *personal relationship* with God is the "flesh," which gives the total being LIFE.

"Our Father" says it all. God exists Eternally—an all powerful, personal God who is the loving Father of all. God is not a person, but He is personal. God IS, therefore I am. As we meditate on the words "Our Father," life is not commonplace but sacred and holy. "Our Father" makes it possible to "pray without ceasing"; for when we practice the Presence of God we have Divine awareness, and know Divine adjustment in all that comes to mind. Error is dispelled and appearances are cast aside, for we know that in and through all of life is "Our Father"—God, the Good, whose Omnipresent Spirit pervades the universe.

Such is the consciousness of Jesus the Wayshower. The Apostle Paul declares that it must also be our conscious goal and attainment if we are to grow "up into Christ." Realization of "Our Father" is the spiritual prescription or treatment which leads us to attain growth and unfold our divinity.

We each have a responsibility to lift the race consciousness through an awareness of "Our Father" NOW. The Psalmist says, "God is our refuge and strength . . . A VERY PRESENT HELP in trouble." (Ps. 46:1) His help is pressing through appearances. His help fills the earth NOW, according to our level of awareness and acceptance. There is great Creative Power in this present moment, this NOW.

When Jesus taught "Our Father, WHO ART IN HEAVEN," he was relating the state of consciousness necessary for us to fully realize the nature of God and to appropriate that which He desires for us. Deep within the race consciousness "Heaven" has been considered a *place* where God is and we are not—hence, separation. *Heaven is not a place, but a state of consciousness.* When we experience His Divine Indwelling, we are also aware of the Kingdom of Heaven. The soul makes its contact with the Source of Life, and is refreshed and renewed.

So perfectly was Jesus synchronized with "Our Father" in this consciousness of Heaven that he could say, "What I see my Father doing, I do; what I hear my Father saying, I say; my Father and I are ONE." Because of this perfect synchronization he could declare these truths to the world:

"Come, ye blessed of my Father, (those who follow the guidance and direction of the Holy Spirit within), *inherit the Kingdom* prepared for you from the foundation of the world." (Matt. 25:34)

"The Father loveth the Son, and hath given all things into his hand." (John 3:35)

"For the Father loveth the Son, and sheweth him all things that himself doeth." (John 5:20)

"Fear not, little flock: for it is your Father's good pleasure to *give you the Kingdom*." (Luke 12:32)

" . . . the hour cometh, and now IS, when the true worshippers shall worship the Father *in spirit and in truth*; for the Father seeketh such to worship him." (John 4:23)

"For I have not spoken of myself; but the Father which sent me, He gave me the commandment, what I should say, and what I should speak. And I know that His commandment is Life Everlasting; whatsoever I speak therefore, even as the Father said unto me, so I speak." (John 12:49-50)

And in the hour of his trial when his friends had forsaken him and his enemies sought to take his life, he could say "and yet *I am not alone, because the Father is with me.*" (John 16:32) His personal relationship and identification with the Father was constantly at the basis of all his activity.

Jesus practiced two principles in order to trace the Father's movements and words upon the earth consciousness. He kept his *inward vision singly upon the Father* and the *Reality of the Kingdom of Heaven*; and he *continuously gave thanks and praise to God* for being in perfect control of all Creation. He was finally able to say to Philip, "He that hath seen *me* hath seen *the Father.*" (John 14:9) And he has left us with a *spiritual challenge*—to realize an *expanded personal relationship* with "Our Father" . . . "Verily, verily, I say unto you, he that believeth on me, the works that I do shall he do also; and greater works than these shall he do: because I go unto my Father. And whatsoever ye shall ask in my name, that will I do, that *the Father* may be glorified in the Son." (John 14:12-13)

READ: John: Chapter 14 and Chapter 16.

CHAPTER XIV

Man's Dominion:
Hallowed Be Thy Name

The teaching of Jesus the Wayshower concerning "Our Father" actually comprises a complete body of spiritual knowledge, concerning that which Eternally IS. The Master provides the link between those things which reside "Eternal in the Heavens," and our understanding and ability to relate to and apply that knowledge. Day by day and moment by moment we are unfolding the Christ within us through the indwelling Holy Spirit. We seek more responsible spiritual *knowledge of His Omnipresent Reality* and an *expansion of personal experience* and *identity with Him.*

Jesus the Wayshower expands the knowledge of "Our Father" as he speaks, acts and lives from that state of consciousness which he terms the "Kingdom of Heaven." Wherever the Presence of God is felt, there is Heaven; for the Master has shown us that life is spiritual, not material. It is the nature of God to be in Heaven, because God, our Father is First Cause. Mankind, the highest manifestation of God, has its expression on earth. God seeks to unfold Himself in expanding dimensions through us. Mankind's divine purpose is to *express God on earth.* This is the Heavenly Principle. God and Man are to be ONE, but not one and the same, any more than the light from the sun *is* the sun. "Our Father" describes the nature of God. "Heaven" describes the consciousness of His Divine Indwelling whereby we appropriate the Reality of the Father's Life, and let our sonship shine forth from the Father of Light.

Jesus went on to enrich these truths by teaching us to hallow the Name of God: "Hallowed be thy Name." In so doing he reached deeply into the tradition and experience of the Hebrew people. We find the Name used often, especially in the Psalms, as an act of adoration and worship. "I will extol thee, my God, O King, and I will *bless thy Name* forever and ever. Every day will I bless thee; and I will *praise thy Name* forever and ever." (Ps. 145:1-2)

The Hebrews were not as careless in the use of names as we sometimes are. The name represented the inner essence or the character of a person, place or thing. In each instance the "name" or the changing of the "name" was attributed to an illumined state of consciousness. The Bible, of course, is full of examples.

In Genesis the descendents of Abraham named their wells and cities to correspond with some significant account in their lives. Because of a covenant between Abraham and Abimelech (Gen. 21:27-34), Abraham dug a well and named it Beersheba—meaning the "well of the oath." Another account is recorded (Gen. 28:19) of Jacob's vision of a ladder set up upon the earth that reached to Heaven, with the angels of God ascending and descending upon it. In the vision Jacob heard God confirm the covenant that from his seed should all the families of the earth be blessed. He was assured of God's blessing and protection, and was given the promise that the land where he was sojourning would someday belong to him and to his descendents. Jacob's experience of cosmic consciousness was so great that he renamed the place Beth-El—meaning "House of God." Originally it had been named Luz, which carried the meaning of turning away or departing. When Jacob grasped the Truth of Being, his relationship with the Living Presence of God, he felt compelled to express his spiritual experience and relate it to the very place where it happened. From a consciousness of separation (Luz), he expanded his spiritual understanding and renamed the place "Beth-El," because that which *appeared separate and apart* was brought into the *realization of unity*—oneness with the Father.

On another occasion Jacob wrestled all night with an angel and declared, "I will not let thee go, except thou bless me." The angel asked, "What is thy *name*?" "And he said 'Jacob.' " And the angel said "thy *name* shall be called no more Jacob, but Israel: for as a prince HAS THOU POWER WITH GOD AND WITH MEN and has prevailed." Whereupon Jacob immediately named the place of this happening "Peniel," "for I

have seen God face to face and my life is preserved."
(Gen. 32:24-30) Metaphysically, "Jacob" in us represents our
working in futility with the effects of life. We become "Israel"
when we look to God for everything—when we deal with First
Cause and utilize God-power constructively.

The Third Commandment says "Thou shalt not take the
Name of the Lord thy God in vain, for the Lord will not hold him
guiltless that taketh His Name in vain." The inner, spiritual
meaning of this commandment has little to do with verbal
profanity. When we take the Lord's Name in vain, we *doubt* that
God is all that we declare Him to be: Omnipotent, having ALL
power; Omnipresent, everywhere equally present; and
Omniscient, having ALL knowledge and wisdom. When we take
God's Name in vain, we *doubt* that God can deliver the goods;
we *doubt* that He can meet a particular set of circumstances,
bind our emotional and physical wounds, and heal our
infirmities. When we take His Name in vain, we *doubt* that He is
high and lifted up, transcending the universe; we *doubt* that He
is within us and within all, pervading the universe; we *doubt* that
He is Divine Mind, directing the universe as Dependable
Principle. To DOUBT God is to take His Name in vain. Thus
the Master looked in the face of corporate unbelief, and
declared, "Have faith *in God*"—in the Name, Nature and
Essence of Our Father—"for verily I say unto you that
whosoever shall say unto this mountain (of difficulty), be thou
removed and be thou cast into the sea; and shall *not doubt* in his
heart, but shall believe that those things which he saith shall
come to pass, he shall have whatsoever he saith. Therefore I say
unto you, what things soever ye desire, when ye pray, *believe*
that ye receive them, and ye shall *have* them." (Mark 11:22-24)

When we properly "hallow" the Name and Essence of God,
we allow Him to draw us into our spiritual birthright—*dominion*.
The teaching of Genesis indicates that God has given to Man
dominion "over the fish of the sea, and over the fowl of the air,
and over every living thing that moveth upon the earth."
(Gen. 1:28) Mankind was intended to "reign with God," to have

dominion over the body, the emotions, the mind, the will, and the ego. Jesus came to recover that lost dominion—to teach us how properly to "hallow" the Name of God.

As we trace the initial loss of Man's dominion, we find that we failed the soul test of self-aggrandizement. The serpent, a symbol of that facet of personal ego which speaks to and tempts the feeling state (Eve), was "more subtile than any beast of the field." It is more subtle, cunning and insidiously crafty than any other facet of the human personality. Its temptation to Eve was to become as the Most High God. The "serpent" speaks in the full knowledge that there is a divine partnership between God and Man; but it would have God cooperative and subservient to the adverse ego, instead of Man cooperative with God through the Indwelling Christ. This inevitably leads to loss of knowledge of Our Father, for mind and attention become fixed upon the lesser self and its aggrandizement. *Pride* is the highest wall between man and God, and the last wall to come down. Emma Curtis Hopkins said that *love of honor* is the last soul garment to be shed.

Twenty-one great civilizations have risen and fallen; the fall of each can be named mass pride and self-aggrandizement—a misuse of our divine partnership. "Pride goeth before destruction and an haughty spirit before a fall." (Prov. 16:18) Jesus, by word and example, taught that the humble minded have ready access to the consciousness of the Kingdom of Heaven. When we properly "hallow" the Name of God, we KNOW His Name, Nature and Essence. The word "hallowed" comes from the same root as "holy," "whole," or "completeness." ALL is God, and God is ALL in ALL, the Alpha and Omega.

Jesus also realized an inherent authority and potency in the Name, which, when we identify with it, brings about a particular result. Since he was perfectly attuned to Divine Guidance, he could trace the Father's Will in all effects, and therefore was hallowing and activating the Name and Essence of God into the earth's consciousness and manifestations around him. This is why he told his disciples to do their work in his (Jesus') Name, for he and the Father were one in expression, power and motive. Paul was later to pick up that spiritual understanding of Name potency. He said, "At the Name of Jesus every knee should bow, of things in heaven and things in earth and things under the earth." (Phil. 2:10) The inner essence of the Name and Nature of Jesus is also portrayed by the Prophet Isaiah, in his vision of the Christ before the birth of Jesus. (Isaiah 9:6) "For unto us a child is born, unto us a son is given: and the government shall be upon his shoulder, and his NAME (inner essence) shall be called Wonderful Counsellor, the mighty God, the everlasting Father, the Prince of Peace."

Jesus appropriated the power associated with his Name, and enlarged the vision of the blessing of asking in his Name, when he said: "Hitherto ye have asked nothing in my Name; *ask that your joy may be full.*" (John 16:24) By hallowing (making sacred and holy) the Name of God, we draw from His inmost nature ALL that He IS. *It is the inner attunement and harmonization with "Our Father" which gives mankind dominion.*

⋆ We must remember that Our Father has the unlimited reserves of His Eternal Kingdom to back up all that He has promised us. "Thou art ever with me, and ALL that I have is thine." (Luke 15:31) His Name is signed to every promise; His Name is the answer to every need; His Name is the fulfillment of every right action in the here and now. ⋆

Hallowing the Name of God brings us into the reality of Omnipresence and gives us dominion over every appearance. Jesus referred to this when he told the Seventy, "Behold, I give unto you power to tread on serpents and scorpions, and over all the power of the enemy; and nothing shall by any means hurt you. Notwithstanding, in this rejoice not, that the spirits are subject unto you (that you are able to declare your dominion); but rather rejoice, because YOUR NAMES are written in Heaven." (Luke 10:19-20) Jesus the Wayshower is teaching us that by properly hallowing the Name of God, we shall also *hallow our own names and our divine nature.* For the Real Self—a partaker of Spirit-Substance—is, as Paul said, "an house not made with hands, Eternal in the Heavens." (II Cor. 5:1-4)

Jesus the Wayshower urges us not to be caught up in the lesser dimensions of life. The established consciousness declares: "Hallowed be Thy Name." We rejoice that our names (our inner essences) are "written in Heaven," where we reside with our Father.

READ: Exodus 3:13-15; Ps. 72:17-19; Prov. 18:10; Micah 4:5; Zech. 14:9; Matt. 18:18-20; John 17:24-26; Matt. 28:18-20; Eph. 3:14-21.

CHAPTER XV

Manifestation:
Thy Kingdom Come on Earth As It Is in Heaven

Jesus the Wayshower, through his teaching and his work, so energized the lowered vibrations of earth's downward vision that he cleared the path to set mankind into a new rhythm—the rhythm of awareness of Life Everlasting. He has caused us to recognize the all-pervading Father—the Eternal Creator—and has personalized that Truth by showing us the Father within. He is that "Light that lighteth every man that cometh into the world." (John 1:9) He has also given us the mystical secrets of a finished and complete universe—the Kingdom of God—and he teaches us how to bring that Kingdom into full manifestation on earth.

When we speak of the Kingdom of Heaven, we learn to see through metaphysicians' eyes. The Kingdom is that pure state of consciousness where the Father dwells, and from which flows the ALLNESS of God, manifesting in the Perfection of His own Nature: Infinite Love, Wisdom, Knowledge, Understanding, Power, Life and Joy. Anything contrary to these inherencies of Omnipresent God may appear as facts, *but they are not Truth*; and they do not emanate from the Kingdom of Heaven. For man lives, moves, and has his being in God, the only Reality, who creates and activates and pervades all life. The Kingdom is here now—around, beneath, above, and within us—and by the knowing of this Truth we are able to live in a blessed state, free from fear and limitation, and in conscious union with God our Father.

When Jesus said, "Thy Kingdom *come*" he was speaking of the truth of the Kingdom as being an Eternal fact and an ever-present Reality. On the other hand, he was prophesying that, even in this dispensation of time and space, there is yet to come a great consummation or expansion of the Kingdom on earth in the future. The central theme of all Jesus' teaching is the Kingdom and its manifestation. He identified with it completely. His vision, his thought, word, and every act—his motivation, and his very life were subservient to the Kingdom of God and its purposes and unfoldment.

To begin to expand our awareness into an effective Kingdom consciousness, Jesus said it was necessary to "repent"—to change one's mind, attitudes and activities, and to come into harmony with God's unfolding Plan for the world. After repentance—or turning around—he urged belief. "Repent and believe"—"believe the good news that you are hearing about His Kingdom which is ever-available, and ever-present in your midst NOW." The beginning of his public ministry opened on this theme: "The time is fulfilled and the Kingdom of God is at hand; repent ye and believe the Gospel." (Mark 1:15)

When Jesus was teaching this he realized that the fullness of the knowledge of the Kingdom was not yet being demonstrated even in the personalities of the men and women to whom he was closest. He taught that the Kingdom IS—that it is Man's true nature to live in the Kingdom NOW. However, without expanding the awareness of this, mankind cannot draw from the Kingdom's ever-present Life and Substance. He longed to draw us away from the futility of trying to "go it alone"—struggling in the maelstrom in order to supply our needs. This is why he set forth the cardinal principle that we should take no anxious thought nor worry about what we are going to eat, or what we are going to drink or how we are to be clothed—the material side of life. The Father knows our true needs, Jesus said. We should seek Him and the Kingdom *first* in our vision, thoughts, and prayers, and all these things shall be added unto us. (Matt. 6:31-33)

On one occasion when he healed a person, Jesus said, "The Kingdom of God is come NIGH unto you"—indicating that a flow of creative energy, Spirit-Life, had been pressed out and was now expressing as health. At another time he said, "The Kingdom of God is AT HAND"—indicating a state of soul-readiness whereby Divinity may express. These expressions indicate the NOW-ness of the Kingdom. Our ability to dwell in it, in the present, is expressed by Jesus when he said: "Come, ye blessed of my Father, INHERIT the Kingdom prepared for you from the foundation of the world." (Matt. 25:34) And in another place, "Fear not . . . for it is your Father's good pleasure to give you the Kingdom." (Luke 12:32) We are meant to become aware that we are Eternally ONE with the Infinite . . . sons of God with all the inherencies of our Father. Man's true destiny is to express on earth the "Heavenly" consciousness, and to live and function solely from the Kingdom. *Individuality,* the God-Seed, is divine, unchanging, filled with Kingdom consciousness. However, our *personality* has not yet attained. It is ever changing, ever expanding into an awareness of all that Divine sonship means. We are individualized expressions of God our Heavenly Father; and we are meant to wear visibly the mantle of our Christhood (the Light that lighteth every one who comes into the world). Paul taught that "we all, with open face beholding as in a glass the glory of the Lord, are changed into the *same image* from glory to glory, even as by the Spirit of the Lord." (II Cor. 3:18) In our moments of illumination, the realization of these truths dawns upon us in consciousness; and the Kingdom comes alive in us. *The Kingdom IS come in Truth*, but the gap between the actuality of the perfection of that truth, and the current level of awareness in the evolutionary process, makes us *look for the Kingdom as something yet to come*, rather than something which already IS.

In seeking to develop a Kingdom consciousness, we see in the Bible an account of a long unfolding process. In the earliest times sacrifices were the accepted way, but were later denounced by the prophets as being both ineffectual and displeasing to God. They pointed out that God requires justice, mercy and righteousness (the fruit of personal religion), not sacrifices involving the temple cult. Beginning with the age of the prophets, the externals of religion were meant to serve as a means toward the goal of attaining the established con-sciousness—individualized, and expressed in a personal relation-ship with God. He has given us divine insight, the optic nerve of the soul, to catch His vision. We are to think His thoughts—to have that Mind in us which was in Christ Jesus. We are to cooperate fully with Him in fulfilling His plans for us in the world.

We note, as the Bible traces the journey in consciousness, that strong forms of legalism also were utilized in an effort to bring worshippers into a closer relationship with God. This eventually brought about the development of the Jewish ecclesiastical parties known as the Pharisees and the Sadducees; and by the time of John the Baptist, the Law and all that it embraced had been developed to a high degree. People lived under the Law. The yoke of the Law was a way of DOING that qualified one for acceptance by God, and thereby an entrance into His Kingdom. Until perfect trust in God concerning every detail of our lives has been developed, we will have our times of living under the Law—striving to work things out for ourselves.

Jesus said that the Law and the teaching of the prophets should not be destroyed, but expanded, refined and fulfilled in a higher way. His way was the way of *abiding* in the Presence of God. It was a way of BEING, not a way of DOING. His Gospel superseded and transcended the Law. He taught us to develop our awareness and realization of Omnipresence FIRST; and having attained that consciousness of the Kingdom, God will be able to manifest as supply, as health, as harmony, as peace, as joy, as Life. The Kingdom of Heaven is the realm of Divine ideas, producing their expression in perfect harmony. "For the Kingdom of God is not meat and drink; but righteousness, and peace and joy in the Holy Spirit." (Rom. 14:17) We shall be guided to do *His* works. (John 6:29, 9:3, 14:12)

As vision and thought patterns are changed, we come out of the realm of carnal ideas and are able to enter the realm of Divine ideas. There is no duality in Spirit. Jesus said, "Every kingdom divided against itself is brought to desolation." (Luke 11:17) We begin to establish an attitude of Oneness with the Father.

Jesus told Nicodemus, "Except a man be born of water and

of the Spirit (born again) he cannot enter into the Kingdom of God." (John 3:5) Rebirth is a part of the unfolding process. We die daily to old concepts of limitation, duality, sin and error; and are reborn into a greater realization of the ALLNESS of God, until we finally reach the state where we know that "flesh and blood" (the life of materiality) cannot bring us into the Kingdom consciousness and the flow of its current. "That which is born of the flesh is flesh; and that which is born of the Spirit is spirit." (John 3:6) Jesus said, "Blessed are the poor in spirit; for theirs is the Kingdom of Heaven." (Matt. 5:1) Happy are those who have attained to true humility and loss of pride, who have emptied themselves of the lesser things (the externals of life) that keep them distracted from inner growth. To be poor in the spirit of self and selfishness is to be rich in the Spirit of Christ. Reaching the state where we trust God utterly for everything, realizing that we are spiritual beings inhabiting a spiritual universe, places us in the Kingdom's orbit.

Jesus the Wayshower also taught, "No man (person), having put his hand to the plow, and looking back, is fit for the Kingdom of God." (Luke 9:62) Lot's wife looked back on the destruction of Sodom and Gomorrah. (Gen. 19:26) She had turned away from separation and error and was looking upward towards the Light; but she couldn't resist turning away from the Light and looking back at the cities that symbolized her former state of life. She turned to a pillar of salt, a symbol of uselessness. Jesus is saying that once you "set your hand to the plow," once you have determined to chart this new Kingdom course, keep your eye single. Live in the NOW. Do not look back. Dwelling on the past will make one a "pillar of salt"—useless to God as a channel for Christ Expression. Disappointments, regrets, apparent failures of yesterday, must all be given to God and not allowed to deter our ability to enter the Reality of the Kingdom NOW. The chains of the past are not meant to hold us in bondage; anxieties are not to crystallize within and cause spiritual inactivity. Our soul centers are not to be paralyzed. Paul said, *"Forgetting those things which are behind,* and *reaching forth* unto those things *which are before, I press toward the mark* for the prize of the high calling of God in Christ Jesus." (Phil. 3:13-14)

In another teaching Jesus said, "How hard is it for them that trust in riches to enter into the Kingdom of God." (Mark 10:24) Jesus is not denouncing the things of this world, for abundance of our real and actual needs is our birthright. However, he warns us not to put our trust in them because there is no security in anything but God. None of the things which make up the material world—savings, stocks and bonds, employment, real estate, name, fame, or honor—can give us any sense of real security. All these things come and go in our lives—they belong to the outer world of change, evolving as effects of life. Only God—Spirit, Omnipresent and Changeless—remains. When one becomes absorbed in materiality, a roadblock is set up that prevents access to the Kingdom.

Jesus also speaks to those who attempt to "take the Kingdom by force." (Matt. 11:12) It is not possible to batter down the doors of Heaven by the exercise of *sheer willpower* or by strong *mental activity*. Isolated "mind control" is not an approach to the consciousness of the Kingdom. Willpower alone and the use of strong mental activities are a *misuse* of the faculty of Will. *The faculty of Will is to SET the goals of life, not to achieve them.* Achievement does not come about by use of the Will, but through the realization that we are *working cooperatively with God* NOW, by abiding in His Presence and setting our vision upon Him. The right spiritual activity of the mind is that of *awareness*—awareness of a Finished Kingdom and of a Creator who is Perfect Love, Light and Life. In becoming aware of the Kingdom we may use our creative imagination to realize the Truth that already IS. It is not a work of "might and power" (the will) . . . or of mental therapeutics (mind control) . . . but the *realization of our present immersion in God* that makes it possible for us to say, "The Kingdom IS come—NOW."

Jesus described the Kingdom as creative, moving, expanding—never solidified or stagnant. Thus we can actually work cooperatively together with God to create a Heavenly atmosphere all around us that is visible to ourselves and to others. Out of the acorn comes the mighty oak. The grain of mustard seed, so tiny in size, grows into a large herb. Even the smallest beginnings in awareness can grow into the largest results. Jesus also speaks of the creative and expansive qualities of the Kingdom when he refers to it as "leaven, which a woman took, and hid in three measures of meal, till the whole was leavened." (Matt. 13:33) So, no matter how faint our ray of Light, when we are living and working together with God from this state of consciousness, we are blessing the world by raising the consciousness of the whole race, thereby bringing the fullness of the manifestation into outer expression. For, "None of us liveth to himself, and no man dieth to himself." (Rom. 14:7) When we keep our vision and our thoughts centered in God, and declare our oneness in Omnipresence, we realize the Truth of our being. We are experiencing Heaven as partakers of the Kingdom in this present life.

In our prayer life we all have times when this KNOWING and REALIZING and EXPERIENCING does not seem apparent. At times like these let us hold fast to the Master's teaching about the small aspects (the mustard seeds) of the Kingdom. (Mark 4:30-32) If just one grain of Love, Joy, Peace and Life manifests itself to the consciousness, we can know that we have made contact with the Kingdom. We are being spiritually trained in the discipline of steadfastness. From singleness of heart and steadfastness of purpose will spring the established consciousness of God's domain, dominion and activity in our lives.

When the KNOWLEDGE and the UTILIZATION OF THE KNOWLEDGE of the Kingdom shall have come, what will the fullness of this manifestation be? John, the mystic and beloved disciple of Jesus, put it this way: "And I saw a new heaven and a new earth: for the first heaven and the first earth were passed away." (Rev. 21:1) The first earth is the earth of *material Man*, immersed in duality and mingled with good and evil. This Man of the first earth places his trust in materiality (carnality) and turns away from the Living God. The second earth is *Spirit-*

formed, thereby neutralizing the illusion of imperfection and separation that characterized the "first earth." John goes on, "And I John saw the holy city, new Jerusalem, coming down from God out of Heaven, prepared as a bride for her husband." (Rev. 21:2) He saw in his vision the ascendence of the Christ, expressing forth in purity and beauty to claim his own, through the Law of Expression. And John said, "And I heard a great voice out of heaven saying, Behold the tabernacle of God is with men, and he will dwell with them, and they shall be his people, and God himself shall be with them, and be their God. And God shall wipe away all tears from their eyes; and there shall be no more death, neither sorrow, nor crying, neither shall there be any more pain: for the former things are passed away." (Rev. 21:3-4) God, pure Spirit, is dwelling in us, through us and AS us. In Him we live and move and have our being. The error of duality and separation has been replaced by Truth. The once darkened mind has been illumined by the Mind of Christ in us, and makes the Reality of what IS a present fact in our experience.

When living in this state of consciousness, we find the Spirit of God channeling to us creative ideas, companions, inexhaustible supply, and divine opportunities. In the harmony of this unfolding, we are drawing from the deep wellsprings of joy that no one can take from us, for our trust and our faith are in God. This is living in the Kingdom.

READ: I Chron. 29:10-18; Mark 4:1-32; Mark 11:22-26; Mark 12:29-31; John 18:33-37

CHAPTER XVI

Liberation:
Thy Will Be Done on Earth
As It Is in Heaven

In revealing to us the secrets of God's finished universe, Jesus was showing forth the mysteries of the Kingdom of Heaven. In order to maintain steadfastness of spiritual vision, Jesus has taught us to avoid certain hindrances that would block our path in accomplishing God's Will on earth. (1) Don't look back. Never dwell on the past, for this paralyzes the soul and prevents us from using our spiritual energies creatively. (2) We should not put our trust in materiality, because social interaction and economics—the "arm of flesh"—can fail us. We gain the true perspective when we realize a spiritual universe, operating under spiritual laws. The "material" is simply Spirit expressing in the outward and visible. ALL is Spirit, vibrating at varying rates of energy, with matter manifesting at lowered rates. (3) We cannot force ourselves ("storm the gates") into the Kingdom through sheer willpower or by mental therapeutics. By releasing our will into the Father's Perfect Will, we become aware of the Kingdom's activity in our life.

Jesus had numerous teachings relative to the coming of the Kingdom. In the Parable of the Talents (Matt. 25:14-30) he teaches us an important lesson by describing the dynamic, creative flow from this Kingdom within us, and its proper utilization and distribution as a "River of Life" in the race consciousness. The Master warns us that the Kingdom of Heaven cannot manifest itself if we are found to be "unprofit-able"—if we bury our illumination in spiritual vaults for personal edification, enrichment and adoration. We cannot submerge our talents (our God inherencies), denying them the opportunity to function according to the Divine Intent, without losing what we have been given. Each soul appropriates from this inner Kingdom consciousness "according to his several ability"—according to his or her level of spiritual understanding and unfoldment. Jesus said, "Freely ye have received, freely give." (Matt. 10:8) We cannot isolate ourselves, and stay on the "Mount of Transfiguration" and build "three tabernacles," for our personal spiritual edification, comfort and enjoyment. We must go out into the world and invest our talents—our spiritual inheritance—freely. When we seek the Kingdom for ourselves alone, we only lose it and regress into spiritual darkness for awhile, until we are willing and ready to appropriate and share the Light that cannot be hidden, and which we can *only* use for its right purpose. Spirit must flow out freely in the same manner that we receive it. The troubles and problems which we see around us—what the Bible calls "weeping and gnashing of teeth"—that is, sorrow, frustration, and a sense of loneliness and separation—are often a misuse of this dynamic, creative flow.

This involvement with one another leads us into the purposes of God as expressed in his WILL for mankind. His Cosmic Will is defined by Paul in his letter to the Ephesians. "Having made known unto us the mystery of His WILL . . . that in the dispensation of the *fullness of time* He might GATHER TOGETHER IN ONE, ALL THINGS IN CHRIST, BOTH WHICH ARE IN HEAVEN, AND WHICH ARE IN EARTH: EVEN IN HIM." (Eph. 1:9-10) Jesus' last great prayer or treatment, while in his physical body on this earth plane, was the realization of this ONENESS; and it was in harmony with the prophets' vision that the KNOWLEDGE of the glory of God should cover the earth as the waters cover the sea. Jesus said, "Neither pray I for these alone (those living on the earth at that time) but for them also which shall believe on me through their word; that they ALL MAY BE ONE . . . I IN THEM, AND THOU IN ME, that THEY MAY BE MADE PERFECT IN ONE. Father, I *will* that *they also*, whom thou hast given me, *be with me* . . . for thou lovedst me before the foundation of the world." (John 17:20-24) *The WILL of God is for liberation from every form of bondage in appearance, through conscious union with the Father.* It is through the power of His Divine Indwelling that the

126

Father expresses individually in us, and as us, who have been born to be His lights in the world. Liberation from ignorance, spiritual darkness, and all forms of bondage, limitation and error makes it possible for His Will to be done *"on earth* as it is in Heaven."

This is the journey we take in consciousness: the "inner" state rests in the heart of the Father, but the "outer" state must come to the fullness of the knowledge of this truth. Paul goes on to explain to the Ephesians that when we pay "earnest" money on an investment, it means that we intend to follow through with our objectives. Likewise, this "earnest power of the Spirit" is our guarantee that God's Will shall be done *without* (the personality) as it is *within* (the Individuality). Paul goes on to explain that the Father will give us the spirit of wisdom and revelation in the "knowledge of Him," as we unfold our consciousness into the expression of our Christhood. "Now the Lord is that Spirit: and where the Spirit of the Lord is, there is liberty (liberation). But we all, with open face beholding as in a glass the glory of the Lord, are *changed into the same image* from glory to glory, even as by the Spirit of the Lord." (II Cor. 3:17-18)

When we envision this completion, this Will of God on earth, we realize that it is not a work of "might and power"—nor a work of "doing"—but a work of *Spirit unfoldment.* "Be not conformed to this world (a consciousness of lack, separation and limitation); but be ye *transformed* by the renewing of your MIND that ye may *prove* what is that *good,* and *acceptable,* and *perfect Will of God."* (Rom. 12:1-2) "Let this MIND be *in you,* which was also *in Christ Jesus."* (Phil. 2:5) Through a mind at peace we experience the fruits of the Kingdom. It is Divine Mind operating freely and expressing in the affairs of men which brings the Will of God into earthly manifestation. We are to be *centers of serenity* in a world beset with the appearance of *error and confusion.*

Because we are at varying learning states and degrees of unfoldment, it is not always easy for us to know, experience and realize that "ALL things work together for good to them that love God, to them who are called according to His purpose." (Rom. 8:28) Most of us need guideposts along the way. We need to treat the "personality" at its current level of unfoldment, and bring it into alignment with the Will of God.

A surrender of the personal will to the Will of God in all things places us in the flow of the Kingdom's resources, and makes us aware that there is no dualism or separation, but that we are one with God-Perfection. This surrender (a dying to the lesser self) causes us to make the right adaptation to God. We find that God's plans become our plans, His Will becomes our will. This is at the heart of Jesus' teaching that "he that findeth his life shall lose it: and he that loseth his life for my sake shall find it." (Matt. 10:39) He demonstrated this prior to his death: ". . . . not what I will, but what Thou wilt." (Mark 14:36)

Encased in every appearance of life is the reality of Truth, for "ALL things work together for good" to those who look beyond the appearance—for those who "love God, to them who are called according to His purpose" (his WILL). It is for us to give thanks for *all* things and to behold the Christ in *all* people. "In EVERYTHING *give thanks*, for THIS IS THE WILL OF GOD IN CHRIST JESUS CONCERNING YOU." (I Thess. 5:18) A thanks-giving spirit is a necessary channel for the Will of God to be "done on earth as it is in Heaven." The mudballs in our lives—our self-centered personality traits—contain within them the jewels of our Real Self (Individuality), which is Eternal, perfect and changeless. Likewise the challenges and problems that confront us have at their heart only more opportunities to allow God to manifest in each situation, and bring about His Own Divine adjustments. We must free ourselves from the darkness of error and limitation by focusing our attention upon the Light of God. We must impregnate the mind with thanksgiving and watch the material give place to the spiritual. In everything we must give thanks because it is the

Will of God for us. Through the agency of thanksgiving pours the Divine Flow. Thanksgiving is a gateway into the Kingdom of Heaven.

As the Kingdom comes more and more into manifestation on earth, God's Will is automatically done. Thanksgiving as a vital key is recorded in the Psalms. "Enter into His gates with thanksgiving and into His courts with praise. Be thankful unto Him and bless His Name. For the Lord is good; His mercy is everlasting; and His truth endureth to all generations." (Ps. 100:4, 5) Thus if we enter the Kingdom through *thanksgiving*, we expand our spiritual understanding and experience through *praise*. The Psalmist indicated that praise would cause "the earth to yield her increase; and God . . . shall bless us." Through that blessing, God's "way may be known upon earth, Thy saving health (wholeness) among all nations." (Ps. 67)

Patience is also included, along with *praise* and *thanksgiving*. The writer to the Hebrews says, "For ye have need of PATIENCE, that after ye have done the WILL OF GOD, ye might receive the promise." (Heb. 10:36-37) The Apostle James teaches that we must "let patience have her PERFECT work . . . " Jesus the Wayshower teaches that the seed of the Creative Word of God "on the *good ground* are they, which in an honest and good heart, having heard the word, keep it, and bring forth fruit with PATIENCE." (Luke 8:15) Many of us have, through the exercise of patience, changed our goals; thereby coming into something higher and better than we had previously been able to imagine. Patience has her perfect work. As this is true on the human plane, it is true on the spiritual plane. As our desires in the material world change with the growing process which we call maturity, our desires in the life of Spirit change even more as we go through the changing process of personality and come into the full realization of our divinity—our Real Self which is "hid with Christ in God." (Col. 3:3)

These are building blocks of understanding, to do God's

Will on earth. Through thanksgiving, praise and patience, the Kingdom comes alive in us. God's Will is expressed in us through faith, love and prayer. If God's Will is to be done on earth, it must be done through us, because God expresses in us and as us. With Jesus, our desire must be "to do the Will of Him who sent me." (John 4:34) There is a perfect blueprint and a mission for each one of us to fulfill. Sometimes it may take awhile, even a long time, for the flood gates of illumination to open, to know the Will of God for our lives, and the part we are to play in the Divine economy. However, as we abide in His Presence, we are released from error, impatience and striving. Our Divine Plan manifests itself moment by moment. Jesus said, "As my Father hath sent me, even so send I *you*." (John 20:21) He promises that as we *abide in his word*, we shall not only *do the works that he did*, but *actually exceed them.* "Greater works than these shall" ye "do, *because I go to my Father.*" (John 14:12) This, then, is the Will of God for us—that we grow into the realization of our Christhood—that we may manifest the Christ Principle in this life. This requires the full flowering of the Individuality—that changeless truth of the Real Self—so that we can understand in both mind and heart what it means to say, "The Father and I are one." The Kingdom of Heaven is already come on earth, but the visible manifestation of it depends on the pressing out of our divinity (the Holy Spirit within us) to transform error into Truth, dualism into Oneness, separation into Union, darkness into Light.

Jesus set the example, "My meat is to do the Will of Him that sent me, and to finish His work." (John 4:34) As with Jesus, we must *view* the earth *with a Heavenly consciousness,* in the Perfection of what IS; and at the same time *work* to bring forth that view of the "beauty of holiness" in the affairs of mankind everywhere. This is liberation, the Will of God in activity. God's Will shall be done (made visible) on earth as it is in Heaven.

READ: Matt 25:14-30; John 17:1-26; Ephesians 1:1-23

CHAPTER XVII

Supply:
Give Us This Day Our Daily Bread

One of the foundation principles of living in the Kingdom is *trusting God for everything*. This requires a complete reversal from the ways of human striving where we struggle, formulate and enter into states of anxiety in an attempt to solve our problems. It is impossible to have peace as long as anxiety prevails. If we hoard, for example, the whole focus of attention is directed on the *effects* of supply, rather than on the Source (God as Manifesting Reality).

There is a corporate lesson going on in the world today, all geared toward learning the truth about supply. We have segments of "haves," who are failing to understand the spiritual principle of sharing with the "have nots." The total attention of some of the "have nots" is fixed on effects, as they falsely believe that God is a respector of persons and therefore withholds from His children. We have segments of people who place their security in the *effects* of supply, to the extent that even vast accumulations of wealth do not bring them peace. We have wars being fought over supply—land, resources, or other forms of wealth.

How necessary it is to return to the basic lessons of supply as taught by Jesus the Wayshower! Our whole life on this planet will be affected for good if we can apply his teaching to our daily living. The secret of supply as taught by Jesus must be learned and inwardly digested.

"No man can serve two masters: for either he will hate (have a lesser regard for) the one, and love the other; or else he will hold to the one, and despise (turn away from) the other. Ye cannot serve God and mammon." (Matt. 6:24) Jesus is telling us that it is impossible for us to place our faith and trust in *both* God and materiality. We either accept materiality and all its effects as our good; or we go back to Dependable Principle, Infinite God, as the Presence which is undergirding and creating All Good in our universe.

"Therefore (if we choose to serve God) I say unto you, take no thought for your life, what ye shall eat, or what ye shall drink; nor yet for your body, what ye shall put on. Is not the life (the Spirit within you) more than meat, and the body than raiment? Behold the fowls of the air; for they sow not, neither do they reap, nor gather into barns: yet your Heavenly Father feedeth them. Are ye not much better than they?"

"Which of you by *taking thought* can add one cubit unto his stature?" Jesus is saying that all our thinking and formulating and struggling and striving cannot produce physical growth. Mental therapeutics cannot bring forth from what appears as "nothingness" the manifestations of growth and supply. Rather, there is a Divine Law within the heart of mankind which unfolds the "cubits unto the stature"—both physical and spiritual growth, and the needed supply for that growth. It comes as the result of an innate patterning in the folds of our being.

"And why take ye thought for raiment? Consider the lilies of the field, how they grow; they toil not, neither do they spin. And yet I say unto you, that even Solomon in all his glory was not arrayed like one of these. Wherefore, if God so clothe the grass of the field, which today is, and tomorrow is cast into the oven, shall He not much more clothe you, O ye of little faith?"

"Therefore take no thought, saying, What shall we eat, or what shall we drink, or wherewithal shall we be clothed? For after all these things do the Gentiles (the unillumined) seek. FOR YOUR HEAVENLY FATHER KNOWETH THAT YE HAVE NEED OF ALL THESE THINGS. BUT SEEK YE FIRST THE KINGDOM OF GOD, AND HIS RIGHTEOUSNESS: AND ALL THESE THINGS SHALL BE ADDED UNTO YOU." (Matt. 6:24-33)

This is mankind's current lesson, coming to us with a sense of Divine urgency! We need a deeper understanding of the principle of supply as Jesus taught it: our *daily* bread. As part of a grand awakening process going on at this moment, we are coming to realize that every lack, every limitation, is but the world's failure to accept God as Manifesting Reality, everywhere equally present. We have contributed to that corporate darkness, but now we must accept the divine responsibility to contribute to awakening the Light.

The Gospels record Jesus' demonstration of multiplication of supply. Mark tells us that a huge multitude had followed him around for three days, listening to his teaching and watching his "miracles." Jesus was always able to identify with those around him at their point of greatest need. He realized that these people were hungry and said, "I have compassion on the multitude, because they have now been with me three days, and have nothing to eat: and if I send them away fasting to their own houses, they will faint by the way." (Mark 8:2-3) Many of them had come from a very great distance, walking all the way. His disciples were astonished that he could even consider feeding so large a group. However, he began by employing a spiritual principle, *giving thanks and blessing what they had to work with*, rather than focusing on the lack. Seven loaves and a few small fishes represented the material substance, the effects of the Source. Jesus was able to transcend in consciousness the barrier which keeps us bound to matter, and to draw from God-Substance and manifest it as "bread." In the eyes of the beholders there seemed to be only thanksgiving and blessing upon the original loaves and fishes, but what transpired (as far as supply was concerned) was beyond the human eye to see. After receiving enough to feed this hungry multitude, Jesus allowed no waste of Substance. He asked that the leftovers be gathered up and there were seven baskets full. It is important to note that he worked with what he had, giving thanks, blessing it, and looking to the Kingdom to supply what was necessary. He did not place his attention on the lack, nor look to the people around him to supply the need. He did not express any doubt concerning the truth that the supply would come from God as a result of the need. As the Wayshower he is pointing out that in order for supply to manifest, we must first "count our blessings" and focus on what we already have. This primes the pump. *We build upon our assets* rather than allowing thoughts of our deficits to fill our minds and clog the Divine flow. God alone is our supply. We look to Him to meet our needs, and then we *rest in Him.*

In meeting and overcoming the three great soul tests which are common to mankind, Jesus also experienced hunger. He had gone apart from the people at the beginning of his ministry in order to attune himself to the Father. He realized that he could demonstrate *full empowerment of Spirit*, and the voice of "the tempter" urged him to misuse this power of God. "*If* thou be the Son of God, command that these stones be made bread." To do that would have been to place his confidence in materiality to transpose itself into the desired element. He would have had to reverse the Divine order of things. Instead of seeking the Kingdom of God and His righteousness for these added effects, he would have been looking to the hard stones of materiality. "Bread" speaks not only of goods and raiment; but also our employment and economic life; our friendships, associates and acquaintances. "Bread" represents the whole material and social scene—all that makes up for comfort, joys and a semblance of security on this earth plane. The opinions of people, for example, can be as important to our lesser selves as the food we eat and the clothes we wear and the work we do. We can go to great lengths to have the approval of others, to gain and keep the favor and good will of friends and associates. "Bread" secured by this means causes us to depart from seeking the Kingdom. This is why Jesus answers this soul test with, "It is written, Man shall not live by bread alone, but by every word (Creative Substance) that proceedeth out of the mouth of God." (Matt. 4:4) Our Source is God, and it is God whom we must seek and serve, not the favor and approval of people.

The "bread" that represents our economic life comes through changing channels. We may not always stay with the same employer, for example; but the employer is not the Source—God is! *God is our constant, instant and abundant supply. He is changeless, "Eternal in the Heavens," working through immutable spiritual law.* When certain channels of employment dry up, it does not, and cannot, affect the Source. Changes do come, for change is occurring all about us. Change appears to be necessary for the unfoldment of the Divine Plan and Purpose. When we remain absolutely poised in the one true Source—

God, the Changeless and Eternal—we find ourselves in the Divine flow, and the things we need come in Divine timing. We do not live by bread alone, but by obedience to the Living Word. So our needs are fulfilled. God is Dependable Principle and He cannot fail in the ordering of our lives. Since He is expressing through us, in us and as us, we can abide in Him, knowing that "every word that proceedeth out of the mouth of God" is bringing us a little closer to the realization of our highest good.

"Give us this day our DAILY bread." This implies that we must attune ourselves to the Kingdom daily, to sensitize our spiritual faculties. We are activating and expanding our communication skills with God, and we are allowing Him to teach us and work through us in a greater measure. There is always the temptation to become spiritually lazy when we find a certain material "comfort zone"; but we find that the "bread" gets stale if we do not keep in DAILY communion with God. The Hebrews in the wilderness were fed on "manna" which they picked up off the ground each morning. Some of them decided to take enough and hoard it so that they would not have to go through the daily disciplines. They discovered, as they gathered it each morning, that if they took more than they needed for that day, the manna was not fit for the next day's eating. Tomorrow's lunch could not be gathered today. A daily discipline was their part in fulfilling the divine partnership. The Father's wisdom provides in the form that is most necessary for our well-being and spiritual unfoldment. Ours is a *supplied life— on a daily basis.*

Jesus related a parable of covetousness and avarice as it relates to supply. "Take heed and beware of covetousness: FOR A MAN'S LIFE CONSISTETH NOT IN THE ABUNDANCE OF THE THINGS WHICH HE POSSESSETH. And he spake a parable unto them, saying, The ground of a certain rich man brought forth plentifully. And he thought within himself saying, What shall I do, because I have no room where to bestow my fruits. And he said This will I do: I will pull down my barns, and build greater; and there will I bestow all my fruits and my goods. And I will say to my soul, Soul, thou hast much goods laid up for many years; take thine ease, eat, drink and be merry. But God said unto him, Thou fool, this night thy soul shall be required of thee; then whose shall those things be, which thou has provided? So is he that layeth up treasure for *himself* and is, NOT RICH TOWARD GOD." (Luke 12:16-21)

Jesus is telling us not to allow our soul faculties to become inactive through lack of attunement to the Kingdom, but rather to build our treasure within, through a heart and mind that is fixed upon faith in God. When we make God our "habitation," "there shall no plague come nigh" our "dwelling." (Ps. 91) Those who are "rich toward God" realize true wealth. We are ever with Him and all that He has is ours to be used with spiritual integrity. If riches increase in our lives, we should not set our trust in them. In writing to Timothy, Paul advised, "Charge them that are rich in this world, that they be not high-minded, nor trust in uncertain riches, but in the living God, who giveth us richly all things to enjoy; that they do good, that they be rich in good works, ready to distribute, willing to communicate . . . . " (I Tim. 6:17-18)

Jesus further taught the principle that we must give and share with others. "Give, and it shall be given unto you: good measure, pressed down and shaken together, and running over, shall men give into your bosom. For with the same measure that ye mete, withal it shall be measured to you again." (Luke 6:38) Multitudes of people far away and near at hand are in need. We have the divine opportunity not only to teach the laws of supply, but to have compassion upon them, as Jesus did with the multitude who gathered around him to learn of this spiritual principle. We need to do what we can to alleviate and eliminate all forms of deprivation and suffering, feeding and comforting those less fortunate than ourselves; for in doing so Jesus said that we actually are feeding and comforting him, the Christ. "Inasmuch as you have done it unto the least of these, my brethren, ye have done it unto me." (Matt 25:34-40) This is the way of "inheriting" the Kingdom prepared for us from the foundation of the world.

• There is a well-known fishing story in Luke's Gospel (Luke

5:1-11) that represents a composite of the inner laws of action concerning supply. It is recorded that Simon Peter told the Master that they had "toiled all night" and had not made "a catch." They were working at the consciousness level of human striving, leaving God out of the picture. Consequently, the supply had not been met. Jesus spoke the Creative Word, "Launch out into the deep and let your nets down . . . ." "Launching out" meant changing the *modus operandi*. They were looking to the channel rather than to the Divine Source (God). Jesus spoke words they could trust because they had seen him express God as Manifesting Reality many times. They had to be willing to give up the usual, familiar ways and come into alignment with the Wayshower. The disciples had met the test of working and toiling all night, but they were straining to bring about their supply with an outmoded set of externals, rather than by making their work a cooperative venture with God. When Peter acknowledged obedience to the Divine Law by saying, "AT THY WORD I will let down the net," everything opened up and their nets broke with the overflowing abundance of fishes. There was plenty left over for their partners in another ship who came over to help them. "So they filled both ships."

Jesus' first "miracle" supplied wine for a wedding feast. (John 2:1-11) All things were supplied to Jesus and his band of followers—bread, fishes, precious ointments, wine, invitations to social gatherings. Even the coin from the mouth of the fish to pay their taxes came from Invisibility, manifesting as Supply. He reminded the Twelve of all this before his death. "When I sent you without purse, and scrip, and shoes (free from dependence on materiality), lacked ye anything? And they said, Nothing." (Luke 22:35) When there was an appearance of lack among those around him, Jesus was always obedient in looking steadfastly to the Kingdom of God for supply. His identity was ever faith *in God as perfect supply,* and not with limitation and lack.

His followers later demonstrated this same constant source of supply after his death, resurrection and ascension. The Book of Acts depicts these disciples of Jesus as actually being the leaven for the Kingdom of Heaven consciousness which was to manifest in the earth. They went out as servants of Light into a world of darkness (duality and separation). There was a great resistance to their teaching; but the Light of Christ dispelled that darkness as they practiced the Presence of God continuously. They had to "pray without ceasing"—to know that all things were working for ultimate good, cooperating with the agency of the Holy Spirit. Eventually they reached the place in consciousness where great demonstrations of inward spiritual liberation opened up to the outward and visible world for the eyes of all to see. By putting into practice the teaching of Jesus and placing total faith in God, Peter was supernaturally released from prison, as the prison doors seemingly "opened of their own accord." (Acts 12:5-11) Paul manifested his Christhood so much that he converted the very ones who imprisoned him. (Acts 16:25-34) People were liberated from disease and mental torment; the dead were raised, and so-called "miracles" of many kinds took place as the disciples of Jesus *demonstrated their oneness with the Father.* The Kingdom was being manifested, the Will of God was being done on earth as it is in Heaven, and they were receiving their daily supply of that "Bread of Heaven" which satisfies and nourishes both body and soul.

The Book of Acts (14:22) admonishes those who have come into the "new teaching" to "continue in the faith." That is, to look only to God as the Source and Substance of all; because "we must through much tribulation enter the Kingdom of God." "Tribulation" means the "trying of our faith"—the perfecting agency of patience through our unfolding processes— that we may be *perfect, entire, wanting in nothing.* (James 1:4) Jesus tells us "These things (teachings) have I spoken unto you that in me ye might have peace. In the world (the consciousness of divided attention, doubt, materiality) ye shall have tribulation; but be of good cheer. I have overcome the world." (John 16:33) As we proceed along the spiritual path, there is always the temptation to divide our attention. We have to return again and again to the "single eye" process, and practice the Master's admonition to "have faith in God." Every difficulty that we have stems from a lack of faith *in God*—an insufficient realization of Omnipresence.

George Mueller's *Answers to Prayer* gives a vibrant, "Book of Acts" testimony concerning supply forthcoming to meet every need, as the eye of the soul is attuned to God. In 1835, he founded the New Orphan-Houses, Ashley Down, Bristol, England. His objective was to care adequately for the orphans committed to his charge, and to meet every need through faith and prayer. Everything he needed to carry out his work (the building, the money, and the guidance) came to him without his ever having to ask anyone for anything. At times the cupboard was bare and there was no money: but he determined to remain consistent in looking to God for the needed supply. Inevitably, as a result of his realization that God would not fail him, the needed supply would come through God-directed human channels. His was a labor of love and faith for over 50 years, and the fruits of his work brought spiritual and physical nurture to over 10,000 orphans. The costs of completing that work exceeded eight million dollars, every bit of which unfolded to him through faith. He believed in God as perfect supply. He underwent many tests of faith, or "tribulation." Each time lack and limitation made their appearances, he refused to take the downward glance, but looked up to God as being utterly dependable. George Mueller understood and practiced the teaching of Jesus—"No man, having put his hand to the plow and looking back (away from God), is fit for the Kingdom of God." (Luke 9:62) He reaped supply a hundredfold from the Kingdom, for he mastered the soul lessons of faith.

We are admonished by Jesus to drop our resistances to what appear to be obstacles on the path of life. All life is creative. All that is necessary for living is being unfolded to us from the invisible realms of Spirit. Let us welcome the lesson, realizing that we are problem solvers by nature. We are constantly overcoming situations in life, moment by moment. There could be no expanding realization of Divine Awareness on this earth plane if we did not have the challenges to apply spiritual principles to daily living. Let us assimilate these teachings of Jesus the Wayshower and call upon the power of God to bring forth the Divine Manifestation. "Give us this day our DAILY bread" for physical and spiritual nurture. Let us attune ourselves to that "Living Bread which came down from Heaven," which shall cause us to hunger never for Truth. Let us drink of the "Living Water," described by Jesus as the essence of Life. "Whoever drinketh of the water that I shall give him shall never thirst; but *the water that I shall give him shall be in him a well of water springing up into Everlasting Life."* (John 4:14)

READ: Matt. 7:7-12; Matt. 15:32-39; Matt. 17:24-27; John 6:15-51.
Memorize: Phil. 4:19.
Suggested reading: George Mueller's Narratives (compiled by A.E.C. Brooks). *Answers to Prayer*, Moody Press, Chicago.

CHAPTER XIII

Release:
Thou Forgivest Us Our Trespasses
As We Forgive Those
Who Trespass Against Us

Jesus places, in all his teaching, a strong emphasis on forgiveness. This is a vital key to the very heart of Kingdom activity. In Matthew's Gospel he gives us his prayer, the Lord's Prayer. He reiterates this portion: "For if ye forgive men their trespasses, your Heavenly Father will also forgive you; but if ye forgive not men their trespasses, neither will your Father forgive your trespasses." (Matt. 6:14) Jesus sets forth an immutable, spiritual law which operates with exact precision. Without a forgiving spirit, the soul is bound in a prison of its own making, and the doors of the Kingdom cannot swing open. Forgiveness, a key word, is also one that can be most often ignored. We sometimes hold our resentments dear, and are either unwilling or unable to forgive.

Jesus understood the appearances of our human condition all too well. He recognized that the ability to forgive is difficult—a hard spiritual practice. He also saw through the appearance (the hardship part of it) to the truth of its negative effect upon the soul. He realized that we must forgive others for our *own health's sake* as well as for their sake. To behold the Christ in another person, especially in one who has "hurt" us, is to bring the Kingdom into manifestation at that moment. The lack of it binds us: we grope again in darkness.

Jesus teaches us that we are bound to whatever or whomever we cannot forgive. He relates relevant spiritual activity on all levels of life in order to bring about release. In one teaching he underscores the necessity of using whatever practical means we can to neutralize a grievance or a misunderstanding, before it evolves into a root of bitterness and tarnishes the soul. He suggests that we first go talk it over with the other person in a spirit of love. If the other person listens, we can bring forth RELEASE for one another. However, if that method does not work, he urges that we may want to take others with us to clarify the situation, those who can multiply the consciousness of love in activity. Knowing that we are dealing with a difficult soul learning, he realizes that even that may not work. So he then advises that we lay the situation before the Church, which means to lay the situation out in the light of the *corporate workings of Christ.* If there is no breakthrough after this, we should realize that we may be dealing with an unillumined person who has not yet evolved to the point of working cooperatively with spiritual principle. We should then love and pray for this person, excuse the actions, and not attempt to deal on a personal basis with the situation. We should work at a higher level. Silent prayer and spiritual treatment may be the only means of bringing about the divine adjustment. Jesus underscores that there are many ways to resolve conflict and that we should use whatever alternative best suits our expression. The important thing is that we do everything possible in the light of Truth *to forgive* the injury, because there is a very important spiritual principle involved in resolving these inharmonies. "For whatsoever you shall bind on earth shall be bound in Heaven: and whatsoever you shall loose on earth shall be loosed in Heaven." (Matt. 18:15-18) If we bind forgiveness, on earth, it is bound for us also in the Kingdom consciousness; and if we loose forgiveness, it is also loosed for us in Heaven and we are set free. We know Divine *release.* It is not the Divine Intent that we be bound to person, place or thing. We are to be FREE, interacting in love with those around us. With forgiveness, we make it possible for that Divine flow of Spirit Energy to circulate in us and express in harmony with God's plans for earth. Moment to moment it really is our own choice.

It is easier to forgive when we recognize another's Sonship. When a man sick with the palsy was let down through the roof in order to get through the crowd and into the presence of the Master, Jesus knew that his sickness was a result of his "sin," his separation from the realization of the Divine Presence. Jesus did not call him a "sinner," as neophytes in the Christian

Way might have. Jesus recognized the *sinful nature of sin* (separation from God), but he did not speak of the *sinful nature of Man*. He saw the innate, Divinely-intended perfect relationship with this man to God, and he addressed him as "SON," not "sinner." He said, "Son, thy sins be forgiven thee." He emphasized his Sonship rather than the appearance of sin and error, and he called forth his Real Self. He placed him before the throne of Heaven, in the spiritual dignity of being a Son of the Most High. In the presence of such Divine Authority, the man easily accepted these words of Truth and acted upon them. He accepted that he was a Son of God, forgiven his mistakes; and he rose, took up his bed and walked. In realizing his relationship to God as a Son—his Divine heredity—he accepted God's love and forgiveness and was released from his limitations. (Mark 2:1-12)

There are similar stories involving adulterous women who were treated in the same manner by Jesus. These were women bruised of heart, with a poor self-image, and no concept of their dignity as Daughters of God. Lack of self-respect can produce illness. Again, Jesus did not condemn them. In fact, *he condemned no person*. He said that his mission was to seek and save the lost (those separated in *awareness* from God) on earth, not to condemn them. To one of these women, condemned by others as being an adulteress, he said, "Her sins (activities apart from the ways of God), which are many, are forgiven." (Luke 7:47) In another instance he lovingly told the woman, "Neither do I condemn thee; go and sin no more." (John 8:11) In other words, he wiped away the error of the past, set their feet on higher ground, and gave the women the new concepts of themselves. He called forth the truth of their divine heredity and let them know that nothing they had ever done in the past could change this, because they had now established themselves in God. They came before him filled with the spirit of confusion and "smallness," unloved and unwanted, chattels of the selfish, ruthless acts of men (and of their own cooperation with those acts); but Jesus touched their Real Selves and they went out in the spirit of wholeness and oneness cooperating

143

with the Father.

When Jesus laid down the necessity to forgive, he also said there was one sin which could not be forgiven, either in this world or in the next—the sin against the Holy Spirit. We can grasp the inevitability of this teaching as it ties in with our divinity—our divine heredity as children of God. We forgive by recognizing our own Sonship and the Sonship of another. We cannot express this divinity until we behold it in ourselves and in others. God beholds and declares us as His offspring. We are meant to manifest and to demonstrate that truth about ourselves and others. We "sin against the Holy Spirit" when we fail to recognize the Christ in other people.

True, the Holy Spirit may lie dormant, as yet unexercised by its human vessel. However, *to deny that it is there is to deny that God exists. A non-existent God* (in our awareness) *is unable to function in our lives.* In such a state of separation we cannot see the possibility of another person being able to reach the level of perfection that Jesus said was attainable. *"Be ye therefore PERFECT,* even as your Father which is in Heaven is perfect." (Matt. 5:48) *Personality by itself* can never attain to that perfection. It is the Individualty—the Inner Christ or Holy Spirit—which makes such perfection possible. To deny that Truth is to deny our own spiritual existence, as well as the Perfect Pattern of the Creator within His Creation. God does not *refuse* to forgive us for failing to recognize our True Selves in Christ; but He *cannot* "forgive," or "give for" us the treasures of the Kingdom until we are *awakened* to the Light of His Divine Indwelling. In the unillumined state, mankind has actually turned away from the Light of God's Presence and is unable to accept what is being offered. *The Divine Law cannot complete itself because it is always true to Principle.* To behold the Christ in ourselves and in others is a principal key to our ability and our willingness to forgive. It also makes it possible for us to be forgiven. By forgiving, we *release* ourselves and others.

"For-giving" means "giving-for." In forgiving, we change the direction of the emphasis from the outer manifestation which has hurt us to the Perfection of God within; from the bruised personality to the indestructible Individuality; from the son of man to the Son of God. Thus, we transform both the direction of the spiritual activity *and* its effects. It was promised when Jesus came into the world that "as many as received him (indicating that they received God in activity), to them gave he power to become the Sons of God, even to them that believe on his Name: which were born, not of blood, nor of the will of the flesh, nor of the will of man, but of God." (John 1:12-13) As children of God we give all the lesser aspects of our personality to our Father and He "gives-for" these mistakes not only the neutralizing power (as if they had never been)—but their positive spiritual opposites. For disease He gives health, for poverty He gives supply, for hatred He gives love, for problems He gives answers, for darkness He gives Light. He "for-gives" and "gives-for" us completely and totally. "ALL things are yours . . . AND YE ARE CHRIST'S AND CHRIST IS GOD'S." (I Cor. 3:21-23)

The office of the Christ is given by the Prophet Isaiah. "The Spirit of the Lord God is upon me; because the Lord hath anointed me to preach good tidings unto the meek; He hath sent me to bind up the brokenhearted, to proclaim liberty to the captives, and the opening of the prison (release) to them that are bound; to comfort all that mourn; to GIVE unto them beauty for ashes, the oil of joy for mourning, the garment of praise for the spirit of heaviness (depression); that they might be called trees of righteousness, the planting of the Lord, that He might be glorified." (Isa. 61:1-3) Isaiah points to the "giving-for" activity of God. God actually GIVES HIMSELF to us FOR THE RELEASE from hurt, pain, illness and bondage.

According to the Law of Expression (like produces like) we actually become like those with whom we associate. If we associate with the hurt (the lesser self of the person who has hurt us) by focusing our attention on the negative manifestation (the hurt or injustice), we become like that one in our *action* and we bind ourselves to the offender. We become in *personality* the very embodiment of the spirit of injustice that hurt us in the first place. By forgiving, we RELEASE ourselves from the *bondage of others* and RELEASE them as well, to their highest good.

There is a great cosmic power in forgiveness. It not only acts as a healing agency between individuals, but also as a conditioning agency for the whole race consciousness. Jesus teaches, "Love your enemies... and pray for them that despitefully use you." (Matt. 5:43-45) The old Jewish law said "An eye for an eye, a tooth for a tooth," but Jesus would have us achieve a higher spiritual law, because retribution makes us become like our "enemies." It manifests our lesser self and thus causes us to "sin against the Holy Spirit." Jesus teaches us the use of the higher law. "Love your enemies...." Neutralize the appearance of evil (the lesser consciousness), for the recognition of God Omnipresent manifests God in action, changing error for Truth and bringing Light into darkness. The benefits of the Kingdom are available for all—"the just and the unjust"—but the ability to *appropriate them* depends upon our level of *spiritual awareness."*

Jesus demonstrated the Royal Law of Love when he spoke from the Cross and said "Father, forgive them; for they know not what they do." (Luke 23:34) The people who put him to death could not recognize him as the Christ, the long awaited Messiah. Neither were they able to partake of his Universal Sonship and come into the awareness of their own divine heredity. Their soul-centers were paralyzed in the spiritual darkness of an immobilized consciousness. He recognized that they were merely *existing* from this state of spiritual bondage, unwilling at that point in Time to appropriate the Christ Principle. They had no spiritual awareness of what they were doing. Jesus could only look down upon them with compassion and say, "Father, forgive them; for they know not what they do." This spiritual act—these words of Creative Life—served to condition the soul of one of the thieves hanging beside him. In a moment of illumination he opened himself to the vibrational energies of the Christ. The thief said to Jesus, "Lord, remember me when thou comest into thy Kingdom. And Jesus said unto him, Verily I say unto thee, Today shalt thou be with me in Paradise." (Luke 23:42-43) We become like those with whom we associate in consciousness. The thief associated with the Christ. According to the Law of Expression, he therefore discovered that he was a spiritual being, inheriting a place in a spiritual kingdom. Not only did the thief enter into this cosmic power of Jesus' forgiveness, but many others, then and now, have received the same spiritual benefits.

One of Jesus' followers, Stephen, followed the same pattern in forgiving his enemies before his death. Stephen was stoned to death by the opponents of the Christian Way of life. The beginning of Christianity brought turbulent days, and these early disciples were called upon to demonstrate their faith in ways that most of us have never experienced. Standing nearby during Stephen's execution was a young man named Saul, a devout Jew and a follower of the "old order." Saul had not only consented to Stephen's death, but he was a zealous leader promoting a great wave of persecution against the Christian Community. It is recorded that before the stoning, Stephen was full of the Holy Ghost, functioning totally from the Spirit of God within him. He did not look down at the intended acts of these unillumined persons, but "looked up steadfastly into Heaven and saw the glory of God, and Jesus standing on the right hand of God." The vision that lifted Stephen above all worldly appearances was so glorious that he described this Reality to his persecutors and those standing by. When he described the vision to these unillumined people it only increased their venomous attitude. They screamed at him, closed their ears so as not to hear the truth, and all ran at him. He was cast out of the city and stoned. As he was dying he called upon God and said, "Lord Jesus, receive my spirit. And he kneeled down and cried with a loud voice, Lord, lay not this sin to their charge." (Acts 7:54-60)

Young Saul witnessed this, and his first response was resistance. "He made havock of the church, entering into every house, and haling men and women committed them to prison." (Acts 8:3) But the cosmic power of Christ, through Stephen's forgiveness, was to unshackle Saul in an instantaneous, magnified illumination of Truth that caused Saul's immediate conversion to the Christian Way, which he had persecuted. He is later referred to as Paul, the Roman version of the Jewish name, Saul. It is interesting to note that the name Saul means the personal dominance of will, or the personality in authority. The name Paul means little or small, indicating that the outer personality has given way to Individuality, to the Christ within.

Paul was to teach this principle of forgiveness from an experiential standpoint. He had come into its currents of energy. He taught, if you love your enemy, doing good to him, "thou shalt heap coals of fire on his head." (Rom. 12:20) "Fire" is energy, and the "head" is MIND (the channel of awareness). Fire represents God Energy in consciousness, a Divine invisible activity that presses from the inner to the outer in manifestation. The law is certain in its operation. We could paraphrase Paul's words by saying, Love those who "have aught" against you because in doing so you will neutralize the lesser by the utilization of the higher. "Be not overcome of evil, but overcome evil with good." (Rom. 12:21) This cosmic action of forgiveness makes it possible for the law to come full circle.

Ghandi's life is another example of the power of love and forgiveness. It has been said that his last words were of forgiveness for his assassin. Ghandi's life was dedicated to liberation through non-violence and love. He acted with Jesus' words, "Love your enemies." Though Ghandi himself was mistreated, imprisoned and humiliated in his work of serving others, he refused to work at the level of his persecutors. This great soul (Mahatma) directed that power of love and forgiveness—and taught his followers to do the same—toward the freedom of all India.

The principle key to prayer power given by Jesus not only deals with faith, but with forgiveness and love as well. "*Have faith in God.* For verily I say unto you that whosoever shall say unto this mountain (of difficulty), be thou removed and be thou cast into the sea; and shall not doubt in his heart, but shall believe that those things which he saith shall come to pass; he shall have whatsoever he saith. Therefore I say unto you, *What things soever ye desire, when ye pray, believe that ye receive them, and ye shall have them. And when ye stand praying, forgive, if ye have ought against any;* that your Father also which is in Heaven may forgive your trespasses. But if ye do not forgive, neither will your Father which is in Heaven forgive your trespasses." (Mark 11:22-26) From this teaching we have another example of the interaction of the spiritual laws of Being. Our prayers are *bound* on earth if there is an *unforgiving spirit*; but they will be *released*, and we shall know release through them, in our *acts of forgiveness.*

When Jesus teaches us about the practical necessity of forgiveness, so that we may know RELEASE, he underscores the work of the Spirit to achieve this discipline. Immediately following this teaching he says, "Again I say unto you, that if two of you (your Individuality and your personality, or two persons with integrated Christ personalities), shall agree on earth as touching anything that they shall ask, it shall be done for them of my Father which is in Heaven. For where two or three are gathered together in my Name, there am I in the midst of them. Then came Peter to him and said, Lord, how oft shall my brother sin against me and I forgive him? Till seven times? Jesus saith unto him, I say not unto thee until seven times: but until seventy times seven." (Matt. 18:19-22) Jesus tells us to let the Father do this forgiving within us continuously.

Soul disciplines can *only* be accomplished by the Christ within us. Of ourselves (personalities) we can do nothing. It is the Father within who does the work for us. It is up to us to receive the Father, or not to. The sequential patterning of spiritual activity begins first with *vision*, which requires an act of commitment on our part. *If we keep our spiritual vision,* the optic nerve of the soul, *on God,* "looking up steadfastly," *our thought will then follow our vision.* We shall have that Mind in *us* which was, and is, in Christ Jesus. Divine Mind will manifest in us the righteous spiritual activities of love, forgiveness and joy in the Holy Spirit.

READ: Ps. 103; Luke 7:36-50; Luke 5:18-26; Matt. 18:15-22

CHAPTER XIX

Protection, Strengthening, Overcoming:
Thou Leadest Us Not Into Temptation, But Dost Deliver Us From All Evil

The Bible presents a seeming paradox in its teaching regarding temptation. The Epistle of James says, "Let no man say when he is tempted, I am tempted of God, for God cannot be tempted of evil, neither tempteth He any man." (James 1:13) On the other hand, when we study the Gospels we find that Jesus was "led by the Spirit into the wilderness to be tempted." (Matt. 4:1)

The temptation to which James refers is the subtle influence of the ego-centered personality, for he says it is drawn away (from God) for its own personal pleasures or delights. Ego is a primary force—some say *the* primary force—of our daily illusion. Though not "bad" or "evil" by nature, it often becomes the tool of personal inclinations and an intense desire to resort to avarice, greed, and self-aggrandizement. Then we lose our hold on the primal spiritual laws of life. There is only a *spiraling downward* into serving self and departing in consciousness from the Living God. This type of temptation, says James, is never presented to us by God, but is the result of an adverse ego which has sought to make itself grander than its Creator.

The temptations of Jesus, on the other hand, represent an *upward spiraling unfoldment*—a spiritual state, when we are ready to put into practice all that we have learned concerning the continuing creative processes of God. The creative principle of life in Jesus' eyes is that Light is exposed to spiritual darkness. In this activity we are working cooperatively with God. We are taking some unformed substance and giving it form, or transmuting a distorted form into a perfected form. Through this process, we are strengthening our soul faculties and calling forth the power of God to bring about divine results.

Spiritual unfoldment does not allow us to sink into comfort zones and stagnate. We find on the path many opportunities for growth and overcoming. We must come to see the difficulties in life to be just as essential and important to our *spiritual development* as the joyful things. These opportunities to overcome—these seeming obstacles—are what *Jesus* meant by temptations. Harmful temptation comes to us when we DOUBT that God is always in control of every situation. Then we may be tempted to DOUBT the power of our own divine heredity as God's offspring, and to DOUBT God's promises to us. We rebel and resist the very situation which God has designed to bring us soul maturity and release.

Soul tests or temptations which come to us during our spiritual journey place before us opportunities to overcome, to achieve mastery. When we succumb to them, we place our trust in false gods:

(1) Service to "mammon" (money, people and possessions—avarice);

(2) Personal power (over others)—the desire to possess exclusive power;

(3) Self-aggrandizement (pride; self-righteousness).

As we are exposed to problem solving, we seek strategies to resolve the difficulty. At that point we are tempted to use personal power and influence to meet our goals. The temptations came to Jesus the Wayshower, too, as he went out alone to plan his ministry. He was tempted to use his Divine Substance to turn stones into bread—to gain the "wealth" of the world: he responded, "Man shall not live by bread (material or social wealth) alone, but by every Word (the Creative Life) that proceedeth out of the mouth of God." (Matt. 4:4) When tempted to use his Divine Substance to display personal power (by jumping off the pinnacle of the Temple and coming through unharmed), Jesus answered, with full soul realization,

"Thou shalt not tempt (misuse) the Lord thy God." (Matt. 4:7) The final temptation represents a giant step in soul development—the denial of self-aggrandizement—the power of the adverse ego which tempts mankind to exalt itself above its Maker. Jesus had the opportunity to gain "all the kingdoms of the world, and the glory of them"—to use his Divine Substance to serve his own personal purposes, rather than the Father's Mission. His response was, "Get thee hence, Satan (adverse ego), for it is written,Thou shalt worship the Lord thy God, and him only shalt thou serve." (Matt. 4:10) Jesus knew that the Law of Love could not turn inwardly toward the lesser self, except to uplift it. He realized his Divine Mission was to bring the Light to others. He faced and overcame the temptation to serve the personal self by keeping his vision, thoughts, and allegiance steadfastly upon the Father. Therefore, he was given the Divine protection he needed to meet and overcome these tests.

When Jesus overcame the temptations in the wilderness, "angels came and ministered unto him." (Matt. 4:11) He was blessed in the immersion experience of Omnipresence. His consciousness was fixed; the testing complete, the bad seeds of personal power and glory were unable to germinate in his consciousness. He did not succumb; he rose to his mission.

Students of Truth are scientific Christians. They deal in the laboratory of Spirit in the same manner as physical scientists examine and log research data. Divine Scientists utilize the same scientific trinity as physical scientists. We go from *hypothesis* to *theory* to *axiom* in uncovering the Truth defined in the spiritual laws of the universe. In our trinitarian study of Truth we begin with *hypothesis* (a temporal presumption) and the first step is to *test* that hypothesis. Then we utilize *theory* (an unproved body of knowledge) and test the *laws and principles of Truth* in the laboratory of Spirit—the personal proving ground. When the concepts have been proven through *application*, they become *axioms—self-evident, reliable, dependable Truth.* The soul progresses from one axiom (proven truth) to another. The Bible says, "precept upon precept, line upon line" (Isa. 28:9-10)—until we prove, as Jesus demonstrated, that the "last enemy (illusion) that shall be destroyed is death." (I Cor. 15:26) *Temptation*, then, is "proving ground of the Spirit"—an opportunity to *apply all that we have learned*. We must internalize the Truth that God is ALL IN ALL and act upon it by allowing Him to "*perfect* ALL that concerns us." Jesus the Wayshower could act upon every statement of Truth which he proclaimed. There are many temptations or testing situations that may confront us, but all relate in some way to the three soul tests that Jesus met and overcame, and thereby set him free to begin his public ministry with single eye and purpose.

The Scriptures tell us of more. Paul, for example, faced similar soul tests at various times through life. It is apparent that every one of us must enter a "wilderness experience" and overcome the subtle temptations of the adverse ego before we are able to progress in our soul development. Otherwise our souls will remain fractured or split in two, attempting to serve God *and* mammon. We will serve many masters (ego illusions) rather than the Christ of our own being.

Jesus the Wayshower was tempted in all ways as we are. He referred to his disciples as "these who have continued with me in my temptations." (Luke 22:28) His temptations are also our temptations. His wilderness experience is a priority for our own growth in Spirit. God's Divine protection is as available to us as it was to Jesus. We must learn constructively to USE temptation as it meets the Divine purpose. If there is nothing more to overcome there would be no opportunity for growth and expansion. We have already overcome, perhaps many former conditions, in order to be where we are today in consciousness. We tend to forget those things that we have accomplished, and overlook the Divine protection that has always been there to keep us from regressing into the error of worldly consciousness.

Jesus the Wayshower gives us a primary way to overcome temptation. He repeats many times that we must ever maintain the upward vision. "Watch and pray, that ye enter not into temptation. The Spirit (Individuality) indeed is willing, but the flesh (personality) is weak." (Matt. 26:41) We must center ourselves in the Spirit rather than in the personality. In other words, Look up, and behold Omnipresence at work; cooperate with the Father and be prepared for the strengthening process to perfect the personality. This principle is protective because it relates us in truth to God. We come to realize that our lives are poised in His Life. In the realization that the Father is in us, and we are in the Father, we can avoid the stumbling blocks of the subtleties of temptation.

As we watch and pray we need to realize our own divine heredity. Jesus' temptations were preceded by, "IF thou be the Son of God . . . . " That little word "IF" casts the shadow of doubt on the Reality of the ALL-ness of God and of our true nature as His offspring. It opens the door to the consciousness of separation. It urges us to separate ourselves from God and misuse the Holy Gift. "IF thou be the Son of God . . . PROVE IT, by using it for your own self interests. Declothe it from Omnipresence and make it solely your own." That is what the "tempter" was urging Jesus to do in the wilderness. It was an attempt to separate Jesus from his God-Self—to live for ego-self and not for God; to embrace duality, to sin against the Holy Spirit. When we give our attention to that little word "IF," we cast doubt upon the truth of our being. We swing from the Kingdom consciousness back into the consciousness of separation and duality.

Jesus said that in the consciousness of the *world* there is tribulation. It is a consciousness of error and separation and fragmentation—of disillusion and illusion—of vain-glory and sickness of spirit. "But, be of good cheer. I have overcome the world." (John 16:33) Because he overcame the world and released the activity of the Holy Spirit, he has also shown us the way to overcome the temptations of the lesser consciousness which cause division and hamper our ability to experience the Inner Christ.

We can arise into our true stature in Christ only by utilizing the workings of the Holy Spirit, allowing God to deal with every circumstance of life and transmute it into the highest good for all. We have the capacity to bring an experience of the

Perfection of God into the midst of every difficulty, and lift it out of worldly consciousness into the Kingdom's Light. Because we are daily "putting on Christ," James says to "count it all joy when ye fall into divers temptations, knowing this, that the trying of your faith worketh patience. But let patience have her perfect work, that ye may be perfect and entire, WANTING NOTHING." (Jas. 1:2-4) Looking at temptation from that Divine perspective we shall seek to expand our communication skills with God. As we rest in the silence, we are being ministered to. We *can receive* guidance and the answer to every human problem. Finally we *can know* that ALL IS WELL. When we are living our lives for God, every detail of them is under His Omnipotent control and direction. We are cradled in Omnipresence as we are poised in His Spirit.

There is always the temptation to sink into the depths of fear and unbelief when faced with an obstacle or problem on the path of life. We remove ourselves from our Divine protection (in consciousness) and lose our perspective—our spiritual insight. However, when we live in the Kingdom consciousness, we are not caught up in the realm of cause and effect; and we must quickly deny fear thoughts and look through appearances. The nature of our problem changes according to our inward conditions—according to what we are ready to demonstrate. It has been said that God never provides a situation to anyone that is out of tune with current need. The challenge is to bring the Presence of God into that situation and transmute it—to neutralize the discord or inharmony—to bring it under His orderly Providence.

God cannot err, else He would not be God. He has designed Life to present us with whatever experiences our souls may need. When these circumstances are placed in the Light of His Love—when we gain steadfastness of vision and thought which is attuned to the Father—these very situations, that appear to be stumbling blocks, are actually designed to bring out the best and highest in us. Every "problem" in life is potentially a death and resurrection experience.

In the power of the Spirit we meet and overcome each test;

then we need not retrace our steps. We may want to shrink from life's testings, but we must ever seek the help of the Divine Comforter. We have been told that "there hath no temptation taken you but such as is common to man." Since "God is faithful," He will not give us more than we can cope with. For God "will, with the temptation, make a way to escape that ye may be able to bear it." (I Cor. 10:13)

By his example, Jesus has shown us the Way. We are learning to live now in the Kingdom. Kingdom living requires that we drop our resistances. We must agree with our adversaries (or circumstances), and allow the Father to bring about a perfect adjustment. "The Lord God Omnipotent reigns" in every situation insofar as we can expand our awareness to realize that Truth, and to bring our lives under His dominion. The Father is longing to bring perfection into all things.

We are meant to experience power and to use it responsibly. We are able to do that insofar as we can overcome all limitations. We have all the power of God at our disposal, but we must learn how to use it through applying it to every circumstance of life. We are being given opportunities daily to practice using God-power constructively—to apply it to every circumstance which appears on our soul path. When we are all truly awakened, the strengthening (or temptation) processes will have done their work, and we shall know the Truth that makes us free. We shall live responsibly in union with the Father's divine Intention and the reason for our being.

The very first of Jesus' parables had to do with the implantation of the Creative Word. In the Parable of the Sower he interprets the mysteries of the Kingdom of God by saying that the Seed is the Word of God. This Word, the Creative God-Seed, has been sown under varying conditions and it brings forth fruit with patience. The Seed is sown (or received) in shallow soil in some instances—unable to spring up because materiality imposes itself and takes away the validity of the Word. The Seed which is sown amongst the thorns is "choked with the cares and riches and pleasures of this life and bring(s) no fruit to perfection." The seed which is sown "on the rock are they, which when they hear, receive the word with joy; and these have no root, which for awhile believe, and in time of temptation fall away." (Luke 8:10-15) Jesus is reiterating that we cannot allow any seeming obstacle or strengthening process in our path to take away the original joy we knew, when we first were illumined in the deep spiritual realization of our divine heredity, and our relation to the Source of All Good.

As we journey along the path of our unfoldment we must not be diverted by faithless fears and worldly anxieties. The responsibility for obtaining the goal—the "spiritual prize"—is on His shoulders. "Wherefore seeing we also are compassed about with so great a cloud of witnesses (the Heavenly hosts), let us lay aside every weight, and the sin (discouragement, doubt and fear) which doth so easily beset us, and let us run *with patience* the race that is set before us, looking unto Jesus the author and finisher of our faith . . . ." (Heb. 12:1-2) We are to be anchored in the realization of God's Indwelling Spirit. Our first desire must be to do His will for the sake of Truth itself, not for what Truth can do for us. Divine Love never fails, and Jesus the Wayshower has assured us that "it is the Father's good pleasure to GIVE us the Kingdom" as we work together with him to do the Father's will on earth.

READ: Heb. 12:9-11; I Pet. 1:3-9; I John 5:3-4; Mark 14:38;
      Matt. 13:1-23

CHAPTER XX

Abiding:
The Established Consciousness
For Thine Is the Kingdom and the Power
and the Glory Forever

The last statement or affirmation of Truth from the Lord's Prayer deals with Jesus' central theme: *The Kingdom.* All his other teachings are related directly or indirectly to that one Truth. The words "Kingdom of God" occur over 100 times in the New Testament Gospels. Even after his death and resurrection he "showed himself alive" to his disciples by "many infallible proofs, being seen of them . . . and *speaking of the things pertaining to the Kingdom of God."* (Acts 1:3)

Jesus taught that the Kingdom has always been from the foundation of the world. It is that Spirit realm in the invisible, the unseen, which he had come to manifest on earth with power. Jesus taught that God and His Kingdom is an ever-present reality, just as the sun is an ever-present reality. Sometimes we cannot see the sun because clouds hide it from our vision. Yet we know that the sun has not changed. It is still shining and giving forth its energy to sustain life. The clouds have no power over its inherent function. They cannot change its nature, and they cannot shut out its light. So it is with God's kingdom. Appearances have no power in His Presence. He is the ruler of Creation and the Sustainer of Life on all levels of being. All life is dependent upon and draws its sustenance from His Life. If the Divine Life were to be withdrawn, every form of life would be instantly reduced to nothingness.

Part of the mission of Jesus the Wayshower was to turn mankind's attention away from the world of appearances and to focus its vision on the only Reality, God the ALL IN ALL. Our relationship with the Father is integral, for he taught that the Kingdom is within us, as well as above, beneath and around us. He urged complete faith, trust and utter dependence upon the

Father and His Kingdom through a single-eyed approach, ever looking UP to Him. In What Paul called the "carnal world" we find ourselves exposed to good and evil—to duality. But by looking UP steadfastly, we behold in greater expansions of awareness the ONE LIFE—THE ONE POWER—GOD—The Creator and Sustainer of all that is. To accept the rule and reign of God on earth (the Kingdom) requires that we come into harmony with Divine principles—with His ideas for His world. The lesser interests of our own personalities must become subject to His Sovereign Will, to life in the Kingdom. Jesus the Wayshower leads us away from the bondage of personal consciousness and into the freedom of Kingdom consciousness, where all things are added unto us.

In his teaching about the nature of the Kingdom, Jesus says it is invisibility brought into visibility. It is expansive in nature. Its beginning activity may be small, even as the grain of mustard seed. Entry into it does not require what the world calls perfect moral conduct, as Jesus demonstrated when he said that the harlots and publicans were entering the Kingdom ahead of the Pharisees and the scribes. Entry requires the kind of faith demonstrated in a little child. Faith and trust in God, and the heart's need and hunger for Him, opens wide the doors. Living a good moral life is a natural by-product of Kingdom consciousness; members of His Kingdom express creatively His Life, which is pure and true.

In this Kingdom, God's people are forever free. Every shackle of soul-bondage falls, for they live in the Eternal NOW, consciously drawing their Life and Substance from their Source. Jesus began his public ministry with "the Kingdom is *at hand.*" NOW is the accepted time to become aware of it. As he taught his small inner group of disciples about the Kingdom, he revealed the magnificence of God's Universal Plan, and allowed them to realize how fortunate they were to be receiving inner illumination of its mysteries. "Blessed are the eyes which see the things that ye see: for I tell you, that many prophets and kings have desired to see those things which ye see, and have not seen them; and to hear those things which ye hear, and have not heard them." (Luke 10:24; Matt. 13:16-17) The

Kingdom is the *summum bonum*—the great goal toward which all humanity is being drawn.

Jesus ever seeks to simplify Truth for us. The people of his day were entangled in a complicated system of ethics and religious practices. The Pentateuch of the Hebrew Faith contains 614 rules for right conduct in life. Its adherents were going through all sorts of complicated rituals in an attempt to secure God's favor and blessing. These 614 rules from the Pentateuch (Genesis through Deuteronomy) were eventually reduced or simplified to eleven rules in the 15th Psalm. As the seers and prophets unfolded in consciousness, again they simplified. The Prophet Micah reduced the rules of spiritual conduct to three: "He hath shewed thee, O man, what is good; and what doth the Lord require of thee, but to do justly, and to love mercy, and to walk humbly with thy God?" (Micah 6:8) Jesus simplified again, and reduced the whole of Truth to *one*— the Commandment of Infinite LOVE: "Thou shalt love the Lord thy God with all thy heart, with all thy mind, with all thy soul and with all thy strength, and thy neighbor as thyself." (Matt. 22:37-40) This basic premise is the *life and activity of the Kingdom;* and *its foundation is the Omnipresence of God, equally everywhere present.*

To present a visual picture of the ultimate objective for earth—Thy Kingdom come on earth as it is in Heaven—Jesus told a story about a boy who decided to waste his Divine substance by leaving his father's house (the Kingdom) and facing life alone. He finally was in "want," and found that those around·him also had left the consciousness of their true home and could not supply his needs. He decided to go back to his father. Jesus gives us many insights as to the journey in consciousness back to the Father, in the familiar Parable of the Prodigal Son. (Luke 15:11-32)

Jesus says that the first milestone in our journey back to the Father is that we "come to ourselves." We acquire enough divine insight to realize that the world around us cannot satisfy, supply or fulfill our inmost desires. We realize that our mind, ego and emotions have not been flowing in concurrence with

God's creative principle, and we long to make restitution. So we "repent" (or turn away) from those thoughts, words and deeds that have kept us out of the Kingdom. We no longer set our goals on materiality or the world of illusion and appearances. We set out to return to the Father.

We begin to use our creative processes positively, rather than negatively in a wasteful ("prodigal") manner. We no longer allow ourselves to divert our creative energy. We are on our guard, so to speak, beginning to neutralize the states of fear, anxiety, worry, rebellion, anger, self-hate, selfishness and unbelief. We come under the direction of Spirit, allowing "patience to do her perfect work." We turn not to people for our answers, for these represent the "husks of the swine" that the Prodigal could no longer eat. The husks of the flesh (the opinions of people) result in worldly anxiety, frustration and despair; but the divine inheritance, as symbolized in the "fatted calf," represents responsible freedom, prosperity, joy, spiritual security, and unlimited love. The more we are disillusioned by the mass consciousness around us, the more we awaken to our need for the Kingdom—the Father's house.

The answers to our deepest longings are in the Kingdom. The supply for our deepest needs resides there, too. The new assignments in God's service will be given as we make ourselves more ready and open to receive. We are unfolding moment by moment to receive, and having received, to be channels to the world that we may assist in bringing the Kingdom into manifestation—to make it a present Reality.

The Father's love, in seeking and drawing out those who are lost from the awareness of the Reality of the Kingdom, is related in the Parable of the Lost Sheep. "What" one "of you, having an hundred sheep, if he lose one of them, doth not leave the ninety and nine in the wilderness, and go after that which is lost, until he find it? And when he hath found it, he layeth it on his shoulders, rejoicing." (Luke 15:4-5) In the Kingdom of Heaven, Jesus says, there is great rejoicing over each one who returns in awareness to his Source and lives in harmony with God's laws. Why such rejoicing over one? Because He loves us, and each one of us contributes to the whole manifestation. We all have a distinct and unique part to play in God's plan for the world. Such is His intimacy with us that "even the hairs of our head are numbered" and He knows "every sparrow that falls to the ground." (Matt. 10:29-30)

God wants to deliver us from this world of illusion by opening our consciousness to a greater awareness of Himself. Paul refers to it as putting on "the whole armour of God" in order that we may insulate ourselves from the world of tribulation around us and build the Kingdom consciousness within us, which is the Truth of our being. It is a deliverance for His Own Name's Sake. "Thou dost deliver us from all evil, for THINE is the Kingdom, the power and glory forever." We are delivered from all limitation, confusion, error and illusion as we ABIDE in the Perfection of that which Eternally IS—God, and His Kingdom.

Jesus says, "If ye abide in me (in the Father's Life and the awareness of Oneness) and my words abide in you, ye shall ask what ye will, and it shall be done unto you. Herein is my Father glorified that ye bear much fruit; so shall ye be my disciples. As the Father hath loved me, so have I loved you: continue in my love. If ye keep my commandments (apply my teachings) ye shall ABIDE in my love; even as I have kept my Father's commandments, and ABIDE in His love. These things have I spoken unto you, that *my joy* might remain *in you*, and that *your joy might be full.* This is my commandment, that ye *love one another, as I have loved you."* (John 15:7-12)

To abide is to *appropriate our Sonship*, to realize our divinity, and to rest in the Father. We are "made in the image and after the likeness of God." This is our *divine heredity.* The abiding state is a resting state. In "returning and rest" we are saved from all oppression; in "quietness and confidence" we realize our strength as God Himself within. (Isa. 30:15) "Seek ye *first* the Kingdom of God and His righteousness, and all these things shall be added unto you." (Matt. 6:33)

Emma Curtis Hopkins has said that "steadfast vision tangiblizes." Thus, there must be persistence and steadfastness of vision to the finished Kingdom—the "Victorious Unseen." Above this three dimensional world we can, with the eye of the soul, set our vision upon the unseen, Eternal world which changes not. We can think, work and live from this dimension and "cease from our own works," "entering into His rest," finding "mercy and grace to help in time of need." (Heb. 4) Our steadfast vision upon the Father will show us that all manifested life is centered and poised in His Life. In this state of illumination we shall neither identify with, nor react to, the ghosts of the past, the agitation of present appearances, nor entertain faithless fears and worldly anxieties concerning the future.

When we read of or experience the trials and tribulations of the world, of economic inflation and recession, of wars and rumors of wars, let us follow Jesus' example and "Look up" to the *Kingdom*, where we draw our supply and find our redemption. (Luke 21:28) Jesus admonishes us to stand firm in the awareness that the Lord God Omnipotent reigns and that He will use everything for good. In the Kingdom there is no lack, there is no limitation, there is no matter, no laws of matter. There are only the perfect answers, perfect supply and the perfect Plan of God ready to proceed through us into visibility. "For THINE is *the Kingdom* and the *power* and the *glory* forever." And so it IS.

READ: Matt. Chapters 5, 6, and 7; Luke, Chapter 15; John, Chapters 14 and 15; Hebrews, Chapter 4.

Suggested Reading: Emma Curtis Hopkins, *High Mysticism*, Chapter 8.